Breakfast with Cora

Cora Tsouflidou

Translated from the French by Dawn M. Cornelio

McArthur & Company
Toronto

First published in Canada in English in 2010 by
McArthur & Company
322 King Street West, Suite 402
Toronto, Ontario
M5V 1J2
www.mcarthur-co.com

Library and Archives Canada Cataloguing in Publication

Tsouflidou, Cora
Breakfast with Cora / Cora Tsouflidou ; translated by Dawn M. Cornelio.

Translation of: Déjeuner avec Cora.
ISBN 978-1-55278-892-9

1. Tsouflidou, Cora. 2. Chez Cora déjeuners (Firm)—History. 3. Chain restaurants—Québec (Province)—History. 4. Restaurateurs—Québec (Province)—Biography. 5. Breakfasts. I. Cornelio, Dawn M. II. Title.

TX910.5.T76A313 2010 647.95092 C2010-903946-7

The publisher would like to acknowledge the financial support of the Government of Canada through the Canada Book Fund and the Canada Council for our publishing activities. The publisher further wishes to acknowledge the financial support of the Ontario Arts Council and the OMDC for our publishing program.

Design and composition by Szol Design
Cover photograph by Johanne Gervais / Zone Bleue Studio
Printed in Canada by Webcom

10 9 8 7 6 5 4 3 2 1

I dedicate this story to all the people of Chez Cora, and especially to my first customers at Côte-Vertu who had the kindness to accept me as their new morning chef.

PREFACE

In May 1987, my mother, Cora Tsouflidou, registered the name of her first CORA restaurant in Montreal. More than twenty wonderful years have now passed, of making dreams come true, one after the other, and of quadrupling and doubling again the number of restaurants in the CORA family.

In these pages you'll discover the artist hiding behind the big yellow sun which is our logo; the courageous *mater familias*, and above all, the untiring orchestra leader at the heart of our impressive progress.

Whether they are big or small, all businesses are born in the heads of their founders, and here Cora offers you a glimpse into hers. This book is full of the brilliant entrepreneurial ideas, paralyzing fears, old-fashioned recipes, and inextinguishable sparks of hope that led the way to the hugely successful CORA'S restaurants so many people know and love today.

Mother describes everything about the beginning of CORA'S with disarming authenticity: her childhood in the Gaspésie; her broken dreams; her marriage to 'the foreigner' as she calls him; her divorce; and how she had to ensure our survival all on her own. In these pages you will read about the opening of our first little restaurant, then of a second one, where the now famous CORA concept and everything that makes up its winning strategy was born.

Without being entirely aware of the potential scope of what we were doing, my mother, my brothers and I put our bodies, hearts and souls into getting the CORA sun to shine ever more brightly. We were passionate about the emotions our food created in people, and we wanted to spread as much happiness as we could with our unusual breakfasts.

Here is our story.

Gestimani ("Julia") Tsouflidis, May 2010

Breakfast with Cora

CHAPTER 1

Ancestors from Europe

I WAS BORN CORA MUSSELY IN SAINT-CHARLES-DE-CHAPLAN, in Bonaventure County, at the exact spot where Gaspésie's tummy seems to curve in when you look at our village on a map of Quebec.

"It's because that's where all the water from the bay goes into its body," my brother Jérôme declared smugly, patting his own belly in contentment. "You girls don't know anything!"

What I did know was this is where my mother Paula Bernard was born, in our grandfather's big, white house, the one just next door to ours, and that lightning struck one of the poplar trees in the garden a few days after she married my father, Amédée Mussely.

Our parents never took the time to tell us much of our family history; but Jérôme's persistent questions brought out that our family came from far-away Germany, on the Bernard (Mother's) side, and from

Belgium, on the Mussely (Father's) side. Much later, I found out for myself that our family tree took root in October 1800, in Heule, Belgium, when our forefather Joseph Petrus Mussely was born. In 1841, Joseph Petrus married Ida Messely, who gave him eight children; two of whom would come to play an important role in the story of my origins.

The first, Henry-Joseph, born on April 17, 1852, became a Redemptorist priest and was sent to Quebec as a missionary when he was thirty-three years old. He led several missions and by 1890 was going from parish to parish, preaching and crisscrossing the shores of Chaleur Bay. Even then, Gaspésie's development was noticeably behind other Canadian regions. When Henry-Joseph met Premier Honoré Mercier, who was also the Member of the Legislative Assembly for Bonaventure County, the latter appealed to him to convince people from Belgium to immigrate to Gaspésie. Mercier, who'd just created and then assumed control of the Ministry of Agriculture and Colonization, firmly believed that Gaspésie had to clear its land in order to make things easier for the settlers. So he'd started establishing a road about fifteen kilometres to the north of Chaleur Bay. Attracted by the notion of colonization, Henry-Joseph left his congregation. Minister Mercier not only gave him the task of founding a village north of Caplan, but also promised to subsidize a future flax mill. Henry-Joseph returned to his native Belgium to recruit families;

several were swayed by his speeches regarding the prosperity of the new continent. Eventually he returned to Gaspésie where he founded a community, along with the few colonists who had already settled on Route 7, north of Caplan.

***

Enticed by the North American success described to him by his brother Henry-Joseph, Charles Mussely, our second hero, and my great-grandfather, left Belgium in April 1891, leaving behind his wife, Philomène Van Zandweghe, and their five children. He was accompanied by two of his brothers, Auguste and Firmin, and by a group of friends consisting of a baker, a carpenter, a butcher, a notary, and several Belgian farmers. Once they arrived in Gaspésie, these immigrants joined Henry-Joseph's community and built a large house that would also accommodate the first church in the new village, which was then known as Musselyville.

A year later, Philomène prepared to join her husband with the children, Augusta, Maria, Bertha, Rachel and little Georges, my future grandfather, then seven years old. A few other families came over on the same sailing.

The group of Belgians left Anvers on a ferry bound for England on June 29. They arrived in Liverpool the next day and from there embarked upon the *S. S. Oregon*, en route for Canada and eventually docked in the port of Quebec on July 12. The Belgian passengers then travelled by train to Dalhousie, New Brunswick, crossed Chaleur Bay on a barge the next day, and disembarked in Rivière Caplan on July 14. They completed the remainder of the journey via horse-drawn that day, travelling inland to the new village of Musselyville.

Late in 1891, a scandal brought an end to Honoré Mercier's government, and it was discovered that the funds Henry-Joseph was expecting for his flax mill, the promise of which had been used to attract the Belgians, had disappeared. Instead, the new colonists would have to clear the thick forests themselves in order to build houses on this land they now called "Hell."

Distressed by this turn of events, Henry-Joseph left Gaspésie in 1895 and went to join his uncles, who were also priests, in Falls River, Massachusetts. After he left, many of the founding families that had also settled in Musselyville (which had been renamed Saint-Alphonse-de-Caplan) also departed Gaspésie, returning to Belgium or immigrating to the United States.

But Charles, my great-grandfather, was persistent and determined. Since he already had a house to shelter his family, he chose to remain in Gaspésie. His son, little Georges, grew up on the farm and became a handsome young man. In September 1913, Georges married Cora Pratte, who was also the daughter of settlers. In 1919 the young couple's fourth child, my father, Amédée Rodolphe was born. When he was twelve years old, his parents left Gaspésie to settle in Timmins, Ontario, where many people from Gaspésie had already gone, attracted by the abundance of mining jobs.

However, in 1942, when he was 21, my father returned to Gaspésie and married Paula, the most beautiful of my maternal grandfather Frédéric Bernard's nine daughters.

Aunt Olivette told us his story. He was an orphan whose father, a cod fisherman, had gone out to sea and never returned, and that, when he was about fourteen and already working in a sawmill, he'd gotten his arm caught up to the shoulder in a kind of mechanical wringer that flattened wood. This explained why one of his arms was made of fabric, and why he had to move it with the other. Despite his handicap Granddad Frédéric married Joséphine Leblanc, a teacher from Carleton, and would later become Caplan's sheriff and an authorized dealer of John Deere farm equipment.

Even today, I still remember the heavy machinery that was always on display in his yard. It looked like its job was to watch over the sheriff's nine daughters. Nonetheless, the beauties slipped away one by one, following unlikely princes; although, in my opinion, my mother found the best one of them. Our chatty aunts used to say that my mother gave in because of the beautiful white collars on my father's starched shirts. And because back then his whole wardrobe indicated a certain kind of affluence it was hard to say "no" to in 1940.

"Maybe his money comes from the mines and shady deals for those English metals," the chatterboxes implied. "But around here, the Bernard family really needs one successful son-in-law in order to attract others!"

That perceived prosperity flourished thousands of kilometres away, deep in the mines of northern Ontario. Grandma Cora survived her divorce from Charles, who had also been attracted to a life of luxury with cousins in America, by opening a boarding house and restaurant for miners. My father never told us the story of how his mother had to feed all twelve of her kids on her own. And the only photo we ever saw of her showed a nice, alert old woman, fashionably dressed, in the middle of the Nevada desert, leaning on the side of a big convertible Oldsmobile, where a young-looking old man, decked out like John Wayne, was sitting in the driver's seat.

"She's on her honeymoon," my father murmured, staring at the bust of President Abraham Lincoln on the American stamp on the envelope, which had arrived in 1953.

Then the photo was put away and with that my father, who preferred to raise his family on Gaspésie's red cliffs rather than in the questionable yellow of Ontario's mines, closed all the chapters in the life of a person, who, in his opinion, we really didn't need to know.

Although the local priests glorified farming from the pulpit, my father decided to try business and became a travelling salesman for a soap company. I don't know any of my parents' other secrets, but I suppose that they welcomed companionship, since, after they were married, they were visited by the stork four years in a row.

CHAPTER 2

Caplan, My Home Town

"PEOPLE LIKE US HAVE TO SETTLE FOR THE CRUMBS IN LIFE," my father declared in 1953.

"And we shouldn't go around thinking we're going to do any better than anyone else!" added my mother in her grainy *mater dolorosa* voice.

And we would listen to them, with all of our nine, six, four and two years of age. We listened to her because she suffered like a martyr, wrapping bandages soaked in boiling water and bleach around her eczema-devoured fingers; and we listened to him because he brought home the money we needed for butter and shoes, after travelling across the peninsula to sell his English bosses' little squares of soap. As children, we marinated in that water for ailing hands, bouncing back and forth between Granddad Frédéric and his missing arm, and my mother's gaggle of sisters who were always frightening us with stories about the bogeyman who lurked on the roofs of the houses where unruly Gaspésien children lived.

Religious authority was often the object of Mom's complaining; she talked about the obligation to have children so the priest wouldn't point you out at Sunday Mass. In Dad's opinion, the only respectable god was named Allan Watson, the big boss at Colgate-Palmolive, because his pay check was never late and the more cases of soap he managed to sell, the better the gift he would receive at the annual meeting in Montreal, all expenses paid.

"You can't work for heaven and for money at the same time," my mother would proclaim, shaking her mummified fist in the tornado of steam escaping from the pot of cod.

"You have to be content with your lot!" she always said, cutting old sheets into the white strips she needed for her bandages.

Over and over she would tell the story of a certain Ti-Guy Gendron from Saint-Siméon who thought he was the centre of the world with his fish cannery.

"Wasn't he the one they found dead as a doornail, frozen stiff, in that little boat of his after it got stuck between two icebergs? In life," she'd conclude, "you can never concentrate on an idea for very long, without Satan catching up with you."

Still, we ate every day, thanks to the sea, and to Granddad Frédéric who, from time to time, let us behead one of his chicken. I remember him letting my mother catch the boiling hot blood spilling from a pig whose bristly neck had just been cut. When the blood stopped flowing, the pink animal was hung upside down from the big beam in the barn. My grandfather opened up the pig's stomach and all the innards immediately fell onto the canvas sheet that had been laid out beneath it. Grandma Joséphine searched around in the steaming guts and removed a mass of brownish tubes, the sight of which made Jérôme and our neighbour Jean-Marc burst out laughing, as they pinched their noses shut.

"It's the pig's intestine," my mother said. "We'll empty it, turn it inside out and use it to make *boudin*[1]."

"Yuck!" said little Tania, as she ran to hide in Cousin Florine's arms.

Grandfather couldn't stop laughing; it was the first time we'd seen this kind of show and he was amused by our reactions. Joyfully, he shouted for Cousin Georges to bring over the pot of boiling water and he hurried to splash it at the pig. Grandma had a good day as well.

"With such a big pig, we'll certainly have enough *grillades de lard*[2] to last until Easter!" she concluded, hugging a basin of fat against her stomach.

Personally, I felt nauseous and wondered if someday we were going to do the same thing to our beautiful mare, Doley.

***

[1] a kind of pork sausage
[2] Deep-fried pork fat

Sometimes my father brought back cases of creamy peanut butter from his travels among the English. In the morning, we would gobble up five, seven and even ten slices of toast spread thickly with peanut butter, as Mom continued to snore, her wrapped hands resting above her head on the pillow. We knew she loved us, even if she never did get up in the morning to boil the milk or mix the powdered orange-flavoured Tang — later she would have to put on huge black rubber gloves to knead the dough for the bread we'd awkwardly slice the next morning.

The noise level would rise in the kitchen when Jérôme would burn a crust that was too thick or forget to turn the square of bread in our flip-side toaster.

"You must never throw out a slice of bread!" shouted Mom, woken up by the smell. "A little burned toast will do your vocal cords some good."

In 1954, the whole village had the opportunity to get an idea of what our voices sounded like. We were set out like a nice row of onions along the edge of Route 132 so we could sing a welcome to the immense statue of the Virgin, which had been specially commissioned for the national Marian Congress. The nuns from Our Lady of the Rosary taught us to use our right hands to hold a tall white candle topped off with a little paper cone that kept the wax from burning our fingers.

After the ceremony, Mom insisted on having my uncle, who was a photographer, take our picture in front of the altar of repose. But an awful need to pee prompted me to tug on her skirt to convince her it wasn't a good idea. She insisted.

"Come now, Cora, a Marian Congress is a rare event!"

"And it's even more rare to have a photographer in the family!" added my uncle, attentive to his sister-in-law's wishes.

Immediately following the mysterious *click!* sound that came from the metallic cone, and while my uncle still had his head under the camera's black sheet, my mother pulled down my underpants and quickly pushed me behind the flowered framework of the altar of repose. The need to pee cut through me and I staggered forward because my panties were around my ankles; I stumbled over some old boards and fell, jabbing a rusty nail into my thigh. They carried me through the crowd as if *I* was the precious statue of the Virgin, explaining that I'd get a penicillin shot to keep away infection and that Mom would help get rid of the pain.

Mother had already been rubbing two warts on my right hand with pieces of raw potato that she then buried in the garden, promising that when the potato rotted, the warts would melt away. She continued to experiment on me with her wise medical treatments by disinfecting my leg wound with gin and rubbing my skin with a small square of pork rind that smelled of brine. My stomach turned every time, but the pain finally disappeared. As for that awful photo by the altar of repose, I never saw it.

***

For Christmas, we would each receive an orange; for birthdays, we'd get bananas; and occasionally, we'd get an apple – whenever Aunt Hope from Saint-Alphonse managed to protect her orchard from attack by white caterpillars. Little field strawberries would arrive at the same time as summer holidays from school, and we had to pick as many as we could if we wanted to convince Mom to make jam. Several families in the village forced their children to pick strawberries and sell them in little boxes to the American tourists. Aunt Emma even sold them jars of jam, but Mom was categorically opposed to this.

"The Americans already have all Gaspésie's salmon-filled rivers," declared our neighbour, Mélie Barthelot, half of her skinny frame arched over the picket fence.

"They don't need our strawberries, too, to spread on their toast!" added Mom, her bandages waving in the air and her whole body ready to storm the Quebec government building.

Dad preferred wild raspberries, but they were hidden in bushes filled with bees. With his head wrapped in an old bandage sheet, and his hands protected by the rubber kneading gloves, Jérôme would pretend to be a brave knight. As long we let him carry the basket of raspberries to Dad, he'd lead the way along the escarpment, separating the brush so we could gather the precious berries. Some years we got blueberries, too, though they were always tiny and never ripe enough, according to Mom, for the blueberry upside-down pudding. We preferred to avoid the hairy, prickly currants, especially since Aunt Magalie had gotten it into her head to use them to make plasters to rub on little Tania's belly so she'd stop wetting her bed.

Some summers, after the hay was harvested, Granddad Frédéric would take us hazelnut picking, carrying an old burlap potato bag where we'd deposit the prickly balls that clung in groups of three to the tree branches. The nuts would have to dry in the barn for a few months before Granddad could get the husks off by banging the bag a few times against the stone wall in the stable. The little blond nuts were kept in their shells in an old tin can of our grandmother's until she decided we'd been good enough to get to eat some. Even then she'd just give us a few, and only on Sundays.

The taste of berries, fish with *grillades de lard*, sweet pudding, or any other food from that time was never delicious enough to be considered a treat. Eating was a technical function that allowed the body to remain standing, cheeks to stay pink, and fingernails to be nice and hard. We also knew that making meals caused my mother pain. With her wounded hands, she was constantly peeling, pounding, or flattening. Our childish euphoria was quickly checked by the weight of guilt.

We understood that cooking was part of Mom's

matrimonial duties, and that she found no joy in it. This could be seen in the way she would skin a cod, or mechanically pluck a partridge, as she made me recite my catechism lesson. Mom would cook things without thinking and without adding any spices. And she would only buy what was absolutely necessary. So she never got us cookies, or pastries, or bottled drinks, or canned food, or store-bought bread, or cold cuts, or chocolate, or ice cream or any of the colourful cereals that the bluish TV screen would later work so hard to push into our unsophisticated imaginations. Even if our house was located just across from *Fraternité* (one of Gaspésie's first food cooperatives), Mom never let herself be distracted by the appearance of a new product sitting on a display table.

Boiled potatoes, turnips, carrots, cod and *grillades de lard*, beef in sauce, pork chops, sausage, and fried bologna were the mainstays of our family meals.

At the end of August, a few boiled vegetables would show up on the table with some corn from Mr. Bathelot's fields. And once every spring, if the year was good, my father brought home lobsters whose claws were held shut with big blue elastics. Plunged into boiling water, they would come out as red as fire. Dad would put them on a big plate in the middle of the table, and, right there in front of us, with a hammer and a big kitchen knife, he'd get busy cracking open the crustaceans' bodies. Then it would be some party! We'd end the meal happily sucking on the little legs from under the belly, enjoying even the tiniest sliver of meat that might still be hiding in there.

After the summer's upside-down cakes, our sweet tooth would have to wait for Christmas donuts, then for the Easter ham, bristling with cloves and covered with a layer of brown sugar, rubbed in by the hand of the child who'd been the most obedient during Lent.

About once every three years we'd have to go to Montreal to see some family member about to kick the bucket, and we'd stop at a nice restaurant called *Le Martinet* in Sainte-Anne-de-la-Pocataire. After settling us in on the padded seats of a red plastic booth, Dad would order a club sandwich for Jérôme and me to share, and a big bottle of cream soda for each of us. And then we would have a race to see who could gobble up the most French fries.

Whenever Mom's eczema decided to affect her mind, the family would be split up. Dad placed the two youngest ones with Aunt Olivette; he placed Jérôme with a neighbour who was a shoemaker; and he placed me with Granddad Frédéric, who stuffed me for a whole month with bread scalded in milk and sweetened with brown sugar.

I had a great time following him around. In the barn he pulled the milk from the cows' teats and we'd spend whole days picking up stones and tossing them onto an imaginary straight line between the fields. On the little bridge across the creek where he'd sit fishing for – but never catching – trout for supper, he told me how, when he was my age, he would spread cod and herring heads on top of the manure in the seeded rows to fertilize the soil. One day, Granddad insisted that I put heavy wool socks over what I was wearing and took me around to check the rabbit traps. I had to take big steps in the snow to get my boots to fall into the prints his moccasins left as he moved forward.

Sometimes, Mom's illness would flare up during potato planting time. Granddad would let me put the pieces of potato we'd cut the day before into the holes and then covered them with his rake.

"The bigger the pieces are, the more potatoes there will be under the plants!" he taught me, insisting that each piece had to have a sprout that looked like chop suey coming through the skin.

Granddad felt it was okay for children to miss school to help shear sheep, plant potatoes, pluck chickens, pick up rocks, bring in hay, and cord wood for heat. One day we made a scarecrow to frighten off the sparrows and used sticks for its legs and arms. Then I dressed the skeleton with an old jacket of Dad's that had holes in it, and a black felt hat a beggar left in the barn. Granddad planted the figure in Mom's garden so it would keep the crows away while she was in the hospital.

With Granddad, I learned something every day.

"When the moon is red, it's going to be hot the next day. But, if it's all blurry, that means it's going to rain soon."

Or:

"If the ground freezes before the snow comes, it's a sign that the maple sap will flow late in the spring."

Sometimes on Sundays Granddad would heat up a mutton stew that a neighbour had brought over. On the big kitchen table there would be a nice slice of homemade bread for each of us and a porcelain cup for our tea. He would pour the stew into two big, shallow soup bowls and we'd have to eat everything if we wanted any dessert. When my plate was completely clean, Granddad would turn it upside down and pour a drop of molasses into the porcelain hollow, where an illegible name was engraved.

"You have to use your dishes sparingly, when you've lost your woman, and there's no one else to clean them," Granddad would declare as he spread a layer of butter on my slice of bread.

One day as he was calmly drinking his tea, he began to tell me how he met Grandma Joséphine in the spring of 1907, when he'd gone to the pier in Carleton to see the arrival of the *Lady Eileen* from Dalhousie. Both his eyes were riveted on the hull of the ship as it cut a path through the blocks of ice that were still on the river, when, suddenly, a young lady shyly offered to lend him her spyglass. Granddad hesitated, moved by the beauty of the unknown woman's face and embarrassed about having to handle the strange instrument he'd never seen before with just one hand. Joséphine had insisted and that's how the steamship was transformed into a bride at the other end of the spyglass.

"Don't worry, Coco, your grandmother was quite a beautiful machine, too!"

It seemed to me that Granddad Frédéric was the only one who knew I existed, the only one who took the time to talk to me. He's also the one who explained to me that the schools of codfish were attracted to Chaleur Bay in the springtime by the warming of the waters and by all the food available at the bottom. Sometimes after breakfast we'd go down to the shore and he'd explain the difference between a smelt, a plaice, and a mackerel. He would show me how the fishermen would spread the little capelin fish out on boards so they could dry in the sun. One afternoon, we saw a big boat full of cod and plaice come in. He told me how Grandma's cat had gotten a big plaice out of the sink and dragged it outside, while poor Joséphine, God rest her soul, looked and looked for the fish she was going to have for dinner. To make me laugh Granddad would sometimes wrap seaweed around his neck and make peeping noises while he shook his flat, fabric arm. When he was serious again, he would tell me stories about city folks' picnic baskets getting carried away by the high tide, or lighthouse keepers who disappeared while looking for phantom vessels.

Still, we managed to grow up and the kitchen became an incubator where our family was constantly debating. Dad would have his backside on a chair with the rest of his body leaning on the real maple table, and Mom would be standing in front of the stove, churning and grumbling about the lousy quality of the big pot she'd gotten as a wedding present. Even the origin of the name of our village was something for us to argue about.

"It's called Caplan because of the little fish called 'capelin,'" Jérome would insist.

"No! No!" Mom would retort, "Caplan is the name of an Indian, a certain John Kaplan who used to live at the mouth of the river on the way into the village."

"The name really comes from the English," my father would proudly explain. "When they arrived by boat on Chaleur Bay, they were struck by the number of cliffs and they called the place Cape Land, which later became Caplan."

***

For as long as I can remember, all family activity took place in the kitchen; my mother's requests for special favours, my brother's whining, the fighting between sisters, the chatting about the neighbours, Dad's late arrivals, and the rolling of the sewing machine, which, as the weeks went by, began to take the place of the husband by the wife's side. We saw Mom dissect old winter coats on the kitchen table. With her gloved hands, she would first remove the sleeves and lay them out flat. Then she'd separate the large piece that made up the back from the two smaller ones that formed the front. Then she'd turn the pieces of fabric wrong-side-up and cut out a new coat for Jérôme, or for me, or for one of the little ones, depending on the amount of fabric that could be reused.

But with the exception of the table and the six real wood Krôller chairs (the purchase of these chairs had been the object of three years of stormy discussions), I didn't pay any attention to the kitchen appliances and accessories: the refrigerator was something you always had to close the door of quickly; the sink was for the awful chore of cleaning up; the stove was the place Mom preferred to lean; and the new toaster was an annoying machine that never quite managed to properly toast our irregular slices of bread. On the counter there was also an electric can opener, a gift from Colgate-Palmolive that we used almost exclusively to open Dad's flat cans of sardines. My father adored those headless little fishes laid out on soda crackers, and as he swallowed them, he declared that sardine oil was excellent for keeping the skin on his face as young and smooth as a baby's bottom.

I don't remember ever looking through or even seeing a real cookbook. Still, my father had bought a set of twenty-four thick volumes of *Grolier's Encyclopaedias* on the instalment plan, thereby earning us a large, free globe, and showing us he was open to a certain kind of education. Ah, yes, now I remember, we did have an old edition of *Cuisine raisonnée* that my mother would look at a few days before Christmas to find a recipe for marble cookies or mocha icing. The cover of the book was frosted with a fine coating of crumbs that had accumulated over the years. About three quarters of the way through the book, a few pages on pastry had gotten stiff under the weight of several layers of grease and flour, an unquestionable sign that our clan's palate was becoming more accustomed to sweets.

CHAPTER 3

Saint-Flavie, Rimouski

Because his English bosses thought my father's productivity would increase if he were closer to more populated areas, in 1958 the family moved to Sainte-Flavie, in Rimouski County. My father was given a larger territory to cover and he was called more and more often to Quebec City, and then to Montreal. In Saint-Flavie, we lived on Route 132, parallel to the shore and the river, in a rented house that my mother hated because she thought it was too big for a small family like ours. At a neighbour's house, we saw television for the first time in our lives. I was eight years old and couldn't take my eyes off the screen where I could see *Pépino*, while my mother explained her condition to a strange creature with a cigarette in her mouth and blood-red, diamond-studded glasses on her nose.

Dad thought that television would be a good

distraction for Mother, but she didn't watch it. Not even when he decided to buy a set and put it at the foot of her bed downstairs in the big house she didn't like. So we ended up sitting on late Grandma Joséphine's bedspread, at Mom's feet, while she continued to rest. We would watch *Lassie*, *Zorro*, and *Marcus Welby, MD* while she'd snore softly or stare at the ceiling. Jérôme would make us his special grilled cheese and bacon sandwiches and we'd wash them down with milk, right from the bottle, passing it from one mouth to the next. Mom would let us watch television until it got very late and snow covered the screen, after the Indian's feathered head disappeared when *O Canada* was over.

At school, the teacher had her eye on me. She'd hit my fingers with a wooden ruler to get me to write with my right hand. The pain quickly taught me to write with both hands. All the students had to collect coins so the teacher could buy little Chinamen from Saint-Enfance Orphanage. On the back wall of the class, just at our eye level, Miss Bigaouette had placed a big box, where she'd drawn a staircase with a hundred steps starting out from a mud floor, and stretching up to a beautiful blue sky that was supposed to be heaven. Each pupil had his or her own little Chinese face strung on a piece of red thread stretching from the bottom of the drawing to the top. Each time a child brought in a penny, they could go move their own little face up one step. When a child's gifts totalled a dollar, the little

Chinese figure would climb the last step and enter heaven and the teacher would give the pupil a pretty picture of a saint. Then another face would be strung onto the child's thread and he or she would have to get to work saving another Chinese child.

On the school playground, we were allowed to exchange the pictures of the saints we received if the one we got for saving a Chinese child was the same as the one we'd gotten for our first Communion, or for completing a perfect dictation in class. My own pictures were stuck above the head of the bed I shared with my two little sisters. Granddad Frédéric also had a picture of the Holy Family hanging from a nail on the back wall of his stable in Caplan.

"It's for fertility," he'd explained. "The Baby Jesus takes care of animals, just like he takes care of people."

***

One day, Aunt Olivette had to come and take care of us; she came from Montreal with two new cousins we'd never met before. We taught them to collect sea urchins on the shore, and that night the TV was moved into the kitchen. We sat at the table and watched it, as we wolfed down egg salad sandwiches.

One fine morning, when she felt the cold attacking our village, our aunt hung a little pouch holding a piece of camphor from each of our necks.

"It will protect you against winter sicknesses!"

She threatened to make us chew cloves if we dared remove the scapular hanging from the same string.

Aunt Olivette also taught us her famous recipe for cold syrup. She quickly cut onions into thick slices (she sliced quickly because onions made her cry) and then she put them in a jar filled with honey. Then she put the jar on the sunny window ledge, just above the sink. When the onion slices became transparent, she added a couple of soup spoons of gin. And the mixture would be given to whoever coughed first, despite the pepper sprinkled in our wool socks every morning.

***

In 1959, Maurice Duplessis died and my mother got better. She started to make shortbread cookies for Christmas again, and donuts, and meat pies, and little mocha cookies covered with toasted coconut and vanilla or chocolate icing. One winter, she crossed the street to give a plate of cookies to the Smith family — it was the first time that she'd spoken to them. They immediately invited us into their big living room to hear their daughter Gracia play piano. They gave us candy canes and Jérôme took several at once. Mom reprimanded him gently, like Dr. Welby's wife on TV. I wondered how she could have changed so much, and I thought to myself that she must be completely back to normal now.

CHAPTER 4

Sainte-Foy, the Quebec Suburbs

"TRY TO LEARN ENGLISH AND SECRETARIAL SKILLS," MY father declared in 1960 when I wanted to enrol in the classical courses at school in Sainte-Foy. "Philosophy, my dear girl, is nothing but castles in the clouds; you'd be better off learning something more practical and becoming a good bilingual secretary!"

By this time we were living on a nice street. Our yard ran right into our neighbour's and her little chihuahua dug up the sprouting flowers my mother had planted with her new flowered cotton gloves. My father was a "district manager" and his company was going to give each of his children a nicely wrapped gift for Christmas.

Once again, the kitchen was the biggest room in the new house. From the window over the sink, one day I saw our neighbour dunking an apple on a thin stick into a bright red liquid that was steaming in a pot on the stove.

"It's a candy apple," Jérôme explained, since he'd already eaten one at his school, Jean-XXIII. "In September, it's the custom around here to make candy apples."

In the living room, my mother was talking with her sister-in-law Juliette. At the age of forty-five, Juliette was taking painting lessons. Since all her children were in school, twice a week she went to the basement of Saint-Nazareth church, where she painted with gouache under the supervision of a real painter. Mom told her she was going to find out about macramé or pottery classes. She wanted to make some friends and talk about her own plans, like decorating the living room and buying the nice rocking chair she'd seen in the Eaton's catalogue.

Then Aunt Juliette explained how she could make her skin look younger. And that's why Mom covered her face with a mask made from egg yolk and crushed peaches. Other days she would spread fresh tomato puree on her cheeks and place trimmed slices of cucumber on her eyelids.

One Sunday, with a pancake flipper in her hand, she asked my father for a car.

"A car of my own! For me to get around in," she insisted strangely.

Anyone could have spotted the big YES that immediately appeared in the pink valleys of Dad's face, delighted that his wife seemed to be feeling so good.

Still, a few days later, the red syrup for candy

apples crystallized too much or stuck to the bottom of the pan and my mother lost her temper with Jérôme and with me, and even with the two little ones who were at the table dressing paper dolls.

"Why is life so hard?" screamed my mother, talking to the invisible psychologists in the kitchen. "I have no friends, no help, and I'm far from my home in Caplan. I hate these suburbs where the houses are so close together the neighbours can hear us fart. I hate their schools, their children, and the way they waste apples!"

Dazed, we followed behind her as she ran screaming through the house, and then watched her body dive back under the Kennedy-pink bedspread with the two white cotton angels in the centre.

In the girls' room, where Jérôme was kneeling in front of the statue of the Immaculate Conception, we prayed that the sickness wouldn't take over Mom's body again.

Dad came back from Québec City and tried to console her. He suggested they call Aunt Olivette or invite Granddad Frédéric to come spend the winter with us, and with her especially.

When my grandfather finally arrived, he tried to entertain us by telling us the story of the Micmacs, the first people to inhabit the Gaspésie peninsula.

"And," he added, "the name *Gaspésie* comes from the Micmac word *gachepeg*, which means 'the place where the earth ends.'"

"Granddad, why can't our holy pictures cure Mom?"

"Gaspésie," Granddad continued, "is like a point sticking out in..."

"Tell us, Granddad, can eczema be cured?"

My grandfather replied by continuing with the story of how the Micmacs met Jacques Cartier, on his first visit in 1534. Then, throwing an old bedspread over his shoulders, Granddad began to parade down the hallway. He was pretending to be Donnacona, the great Micmac chief, who had protested against Cartier's taking over the land and putting up his famous cross on the Gaspé cliff. We followed our grandfather into Mom's room. Jérôme became Donnacona's eldest son and had to hold the lance while the chief pulled down the imaginary cross from the center of my parents' bed. Designated "the other son," I had to lift the bedspread when it was time for Granddad to ceremoniously pray to the Great Manitou.

When the inevitable tension between Mom and Dad arose, Granddad would move Donnacona's camp to the basement. He'd spread the bedspread out right on the cement and we'd sit in a circle around him. Then he'd smoke an invisible peace pipe, through which he inhaled the advice of the good spirits.

"Today," declared Granddad, "Donnacona is going to tell you the story of a young Micmac orphan girl who was turned into a seagull because she wanted to free a young Huron who had been sentenced to die of hunger, and was chained to the highest point in Gaspésie."

"What's a Huron?" asked Georgette, my youngest sister.

"A Huron is a savage from a different tribe than ours!" replied Jérôme, as only the true son of Donnacona would.

"The orphan girl's name was Méjiga," Granddad went on, until the Great Manitou restored peace upstairs on the Kennedy-pink chenille bedspread.

CHAPTER 5

Montreal Suburb

IN 1962, THE NEW COMPANY DAD WAS WORKING FOR PAID all our moving expenses, and they also made the first payment on the house they found for us in the suburbs of Montreal. We made the trip without Mom who was staying with Aunt Olivette to avoid the stress of moving.

"You're old enough to manage without me," she declared as she climbed into Uncle Nelson's powder blue car.

Once we were settled into the split-level in Saint-Vincent-de-Paul, we went back to eating three times a day and that must have been a good thing for our growing bodies.

With our physical beings looked after, it was hoped school would look after moulding our personalities. However, our teachers were satisfied with simply transmitting historic, religious, mathematic, and scientific facts. Still, my mother assumed we were learning the essentials of morality.

"You now know what's right and what's wrong," she declared in 1964. "So behave accordingly!"

To tell the truth, Mom hadn't done it either — she'd never taught us the difference between right and wrong. And she didn't know how upsetting stories about babies found in cabbage patches would become for her three little girls as time went by. We'd stopped playing store and celebrating mass on a lace-edged pillowcase, but God and fear of his Last Judgement remained at the forefront of our minds. All of my teenage years became one big existential question mark.

Deprived of tenderness and affection, my two sisters and I desperately searched to find the natural law that had been hidden from us. Each of us, in her own way and according to her own needs created her own principles, but they were so weak they often led to suffering. Because no one ever mentioned the multiple talents we each had, we ate kilos of food to fill the emptiness, while our brother drowned his emptiness in the same alcohol as our father.

***

Still, in the new suburbs, there were pleasant activities to keep children entertained. During summer vacations, they gathered in parks where there were slides, swings, and big tables with benches attached to the legs. A young woman would be in charge of getting the kids to play all kinds of games with balls, or have a hunt to find the first four-leaf clover, or play hopscotch. By then I was fifteen years old and swings were of no interest to me. But the playground did give me the opportunity to reach my goal – education. By getting myself hired at the park, I was able to convince my father to let me go to private school to be taught by the nuns.

"Dad! I'll pay the first two hundred dollars myself. You can't say no!"

He firmly answered yes and Mom got busy cutting the navy blue uniform they wore at Cardinal-Léger out of the mid-season cape she'd worn back in the days of tomato puree face masks.

"It's like new, it's never been worn. I won't even have to use the reverse side," said Mom as she made strange cooing noises in her throat.

It seemed to me that the new suburb was good for Mom's health. Or was it just my own eyes, since they now had other examples of what was normal? I discovered literature, Dostoyevsky's *The Idiot* and Gabriel Roy's *Tin Flute*. I learned there were other worlds, other kinds of sadness, and other ways besides mine of stockpiling childish photographs in one's memory. More and more, I was inclined to protest, like Donnacona protested against Cartier; I wanted to scream at my mother that there was more to me than a body to feed; that I wasn't just a plant out in the garden that she had to water and protect from the cold. I had questions, and dreams, and I wanted my heroes to listen to me talk about them. I wanted someone to understand my strong desire to learn more, to encourage my will to become someone, someone good, someone who could succeed in life.

To my great joy, my classical studies expanded my brain and filled it with knowledge. When I was learning Greek and Latin, history, and especially literature, I felt like I was living the best years of my life; it was as if every day a teacher offered the class a new feast of artistic thoughts. On top of that, the school was in downtown Montreal and I met young girls from all stations of life there; from ordinary girls like me, to the daughters of notaries, lawyers, dentists, and even the deputy minister for Women's Issues.

When it was my turn to try composing sentences, I discovered the incredible power of words. It was tempting to use as many as I could, and I tried to distance myself from the shore, like the famous poet Rimbaud in his drunken boat.

CHAPTER 6

The Greek Marriage

MY SUDDEN INTEREST IN BEAUTY MANAGED TO KEEP MY FEET on the ground until 1967, when it led me to fall for a superb Greek profile and the young man it belonged to. I soon found my first child inhabiting the fertile cavity inside me.

"The more things change, the more they stay the same," said the old folks from Gaspésie on the church steps in Caplan.

Ever since the world began, generations have continued the species by playing out the same scenario with different details. I got married without much love and had children who would, like me, search for a liberating balance.

In 1968 my husband and I moved into Montreal's immigrant area of Parc Avenue, and my French physique became a kind of secondary divinity that my husband liked to show off. As he became aware of all the poets living in my head, he also became more and more jealous until the annoyed Apollo turned into Aries, God of War. I didn't speak Greek well enough; I spent too much time reading; I'd never eaten squid; I liked to write and women weren't allowed to do that; I didn't swaddle my baby properly in order for his limbs to get strong the way they were supposed to; or I wasn't good at boiling the dried chamomile branches for my bed-ridden mother-in-law.

Despite his handsome face, my husband was also part of the worn out fabric of this civilisation that had been forced to move too often. Paradoxically, under the Greek yoke, beautiful Parc Avenue lost its classical beauty. By then, I didn't notice anything — no poetry, no music, no theatre, not even the sunny sound of the first day of spring. I spent whole days rocking Titan, my baby; it made me feel much better, and those rare moments of happiness made me certain that life could indeed love me, so ultimately I accepted things the way they were.

Late some afternoons, the baby's babbling even managed to brighten up our dark apartment on Jeanne-Mance Street, and my son and I would dance, wrapped up in a love that was indefinable, untouchable, and disturbing to a jealous husband.

Finally giving in to the necessities of daily life, I agreed to purchase a few lamps, a vacuum cleaner, some kitchen utensils, and dishes to furnish the apartment. Then one day, when we were having a picnic on

Mont Royal's beloved, velvety grass, little Titan took his first steps. At nearly the same instant, I thought I felt a little girl dig into the quilted darkness inside me. There was still so much goodness in the world, so many little hopes sprinkled into our lives like little bits of stars or diamonds strewn in river beds.

My daughter Julia appeared, pink and screaming, breaking through the torrid July heat; she became a peony, a daisy, the most beautiful flower in all my imaginary gardens. Then, as life was doling out its skinned knees, its first vaccinations, cough syrups and chickenpox, a third little one within me discovered the birth canal. Baby Nicholas arrived, glorious with grace, and filled my heart with even more blessed assurance. The children grew up surrounded by this new hope and they could feel its effects.

Outside, Parc Avenue continued to change. Still, Planet Athens taught me English, modern Greek, and the shrill language of Quebecois tears. And, to my great surprise, all the basics of an extraordinary cooking style that used olive oil. I discovered eggplant, zucchini, dill, artichokes, lentils, and big beans in fresh tomato puree. I flattened bread dough into thin pitas. I discovered the magic of home-made yogurt.

At the age of three, both of my sons and my daughter were dipped into the big pot used in Orthodox baptisms, in front of the whole Greek family, decked out in their Sunday best. Every time, it was a huge party, where the child's name – whether it came from the grandfather, the grandmother, or the uncle, on their father's side – was made official. During my daughter's ceremony, her godfather, one of the men of the clan, gave her five gold *lira* so, when the time came, she would be able to find herself a good husband.

The Tsouflidis children and I, Mrs. Tsouflidou (in the Greek language, the spelling of the wife's name – the woman belonging to the man – is changed since it follows the genitive case declension to show possession) resisted this crossroads of mentalities as best as we could. And, even if it was artificial, it gave me a certain distinctive social status that was difficult to ignore in 1975.

The marital odyssey lasted thirteen long years and allowed me to master all the tasks that fell to a woman who stayed at home. Thank God, it was the good health of my hands that allowed me to survive the Greek trauma by sewing, knitting, scrubbing, and cooking. With a lot of practice, I became quite adept at unravelling the old Greek cardigan and turning it into cute little smocks for my children.

After wallowing pleasantly in all the sins of the New Testament, my husband decided to become a strict follower of the Old Testament God. Therefore, I had to stand while he ate, destroy all the books I possessed, and, the worst thing of all for me, burn all the personal writing I'd done since I was a child. But then he went too far: he sentenced me to live life as nothing but an extension of himself, with no brain, no desires and, above all, no moral judgment. Then, without even realising he was the one who'd turned off the central heat, the master began to grumble about how cold his secondary residence was.

Now that I also had to mentally give up the bewitching rhymes in the poems I'd learned at school, I realised that my only hope for escape was found in my terribly useful hands, hands that possessed all the concentrated energy of hundreds of generations of women who had come before me. Still, I was far from imagining that cooking was where I would discover so many basic truths.

The marriage unavoidably turned to vinegar. And when my brain was finally freed from the dictatorship, it seemed it had become nothing more than a vegetable that had shrivelled from sitting too long in its marinade. My parents finally took pity on me; they offered to look after the children in order to help me start my life over. Getting by without any money forced me to go above and beyond. I had no skills and no practical knowledge of the world, my only reflex was to do what the inhabitants of Planet Athens did: first I worked in a restaurant, then, I opened my own.

It wasn't until later that I learned this was the same thing my grandmother Cora Pratte had done after her husband left for the United States.

CHAPTER 7

Starting Life Over

IN 1980, THE SLIM PROFITS FROM THE SALE OF THE FAMILY home allowed me to purchase a small neighbourhood restaurant on the corner of Papineau Street and Belanger Street on the island of Montreal. Working over the hot stove for ten long months, from dawn until eleven in the evening, I discovered how much confidence my customers had in my cooking. I needed to be liked, and, therefore, I needed to make people happy. I quickly realized that the little place on Papineau Street represented my first official communication with the world. In 1947, I'd tumbled into the middle of a huge planetary picnic, and, years later, I was still trying to understand why the first man had been created. I had a most extraordinary opportunity to learn the answer to this question when I had to take responsibility for my own existence and for each of the dreams I wanted to see come true. I would still take a few detours before the microcosm of the commercial kitchen would become the centre of activity on my personal journey.

My grandfather Frédéric and Chief Donnacona died together, on the same day in 1977. As for my parents, they continued to slow down and submit to the inevitable laws of aging. Mom had always highly opposed my Greek marriage, and as for Dad, well, he preferred to keep quiet on the subject until he died in November 1980.

***

Now that she was living alone in her winterized cottage in Saint-Adèle, my mother insisted on bringing up the children while I went about "starting a new life."

"Starting a new life" actually became her favourite expression. And it made me think of the long evenings in Sainte-Flavie when Aunt Olivette was looking after us and she would decide the TV was broken. She'd get out two decks of cards, mix them together and settle us in at the kitchen table where we'd build castles that constantly had to be rebuilt because they'd collapse at the slightest disturbance. My mother, at more than fifty years old, began to think about starting a new life herself, leafing through the personal ads in the Saturday edition of *La Presse* newspaper. The children watched her as she circled possible candidates, wrote down phone numbers, powdered her cheeks, and was suddenly interested in the new slimming girdles the sales flyers were raving about.

On Papineau Street, the evenings became less monotonous, too, since I had time to chat with the customers, coming out of the kitchen with a tray of fudge I'd just whipped up, or a few slices of garlic bread for the guy who was eating spaghetti, or a nice lemon meringue pie that looked like a snow squall in Gaspésie.

"Sometimes it snowed so much the school would close for a whole week!" I told Marcel, a poor city boy who'd never seen a snow drift last long enough to keep him from going to buy his cigarettes.

As I leaned on the counter, I realized that the customers' *oohs!* and *ahs!* were not just directed at the food. It was obvious they liked me since the restaurant was filling up three times a day. Patiently, I'd listen to the old woman as she dunked her toast in her tea; I'd comfort the women who'd lost their jobs as they told me their problems; and I'd have impassioned discussions with any intellectual who stumbled into the place by accident.

One fine morning, a young Greek man, probably attracted by the crowded tables, came into the restaurant and, in an English accent that was so thick you could cut it with a knife, offered to buy my business on the spot.

"Why not? In business, everything is for sale!" I replied to him in perfect Greek.

The young Athenian then went about trying to get me to name a price. And, right there in front of him, I told big Raoul, one of my regulars, that soon I'd have the means to get the pizza oven out of the front of the restaurant.

After a few days of welcome courting, the young Greek man offered a sum that was three times greater than what it had taken to buy the business. Good-bye, *Mon Château*! (That was the name I'd given my first restaurant – very appropriate, indeed.)

When the transaction was completed, I joined the children at my mother's. After contemplating the wild daisies growing on the hills of Sainte-Adèle for a few days, I went back to the Montreal suburbs and was hired, in 1981, at a big restaurant in Laval. After starting as a hostess in the evenings, I eventually had the opportunity to learn every aspect of the hospitality industry. For five years, one by one, I took on more responsibility until I became general manager of the place. My financial situation improved and I bought a house in the suburbs for the children.

CHAPTER 8

Mother's Death

IN 1982, MY MOTHER WAS THINKING ABOUT LEAVING Saint-Adèle and moving in with us, in our new house in Boisbriand. Early in the summer, just before her move, she decided to take the children to visit the famous Gaspésie she'd been telling them about all winter. Getting ready for the trip was quite a party. But when the little Austin Marina was climbing the last cliff before arriving in Saint-Charles-de-Caplan, destiny decided to permanently change Mom's address. Her car was in a head-on crash with a distant cousin's five-ton truck that was bringing sheep to the slaughterhouse in nearby Maria. The Austin flipped over several times and finally landed in a hay field at the bottom of the cliff. My mother's face was disfigured beyond recognition and her head hung from a hole in the driver's side window. My thirteen-year-old son managed to get himself out of the smoking wreck.

Titan immediately thought of his younger brother and sister, still stuck in the car. He had to get them out and he did.

"It's a damn miracle!" shouted the first witness to arrive at the scene.

The provincial police were also speechless when it came to explaining how the children survived. The whole village of Caplan was shocked and saddened at the accident.

Mysteriously, neither of the two strong emotions I was feeling would allow me to express the other one. It was as if there had been a head-on crash in my heart, too; the joy I felt at seeing my children safe and sound remained as silent as the sadness at losing my mother.

At the county morgue, I coldly identified my mother's massacred face. Then, the medical examiner took off her wedding ring and gave it to me.

"Another house of cards collapsing," Aunt Olivette would have concluded.

***

My mother's passing ultimately became a kind of liberation. Strangely, in our imagination, tragedy recedes; reality then seemed different to me. Even if my childhood hadn't been a time of perfect happiness, and even if my parents' indifference sometimes seemed like the cruellest thing in the world, I could decide to do things differently now. I wanted to move forward, learn more and get my head above the unhappy waters of the ocean that had made up my mother's world. It wasn't until much later that I'd understand the source of my mother's suffering, her solitude, and the drama of having her own dreams die before they were even born.

CHAPTER 9

Getting Better

IN 1985, IT SEEMED TO ME THE PROVERBIAL WINDS WERE starting to blow in my favour. The big boss of the Greek restaurant where I was working recognized my entrepreneurial qualities and because he often saw me analysing different business offers in trade publications, he invited me to become his partner.

As his associate, I tried to be the best I could and decided not to take a single day off. Indeed, I convinced Mr. Dimitri to open earlier in order to serve breakfast. This meant that, for the next twenty months, from seven in the morning until late at night, the clattering of dishes would become the focus of all my attention. I was always upset by the fact that I never had enough time to accommodate the work I wanted to put in. I would also think of how my children were left to fend for themselves, how their hearts were left alone as I was killing myself to feed their bodies.

Then, despite myself and without really noticing, my energy began to drop off. One morning, it was as if my brain had exploded. With a simultaneous weakening of all my faculties, I was taken over by a strange illness. The doctors said I was suffering from burnout.

"It happens to everyone," old Dr. Bertrand, the neurologist, assured me, straddling a little school chair that had somehow found its way into his office.

When I was a teenager, some nights when I was coming home from a friend's house, I'd start to run, imagining that a faceless monster was on my heels; sometimes it was a wild animal like a roaring lion, or even some kind of prehistoric snake. Immobilised and sick, I now felt like the monster had caught up with me; that it had swallowed me up and was now occupying my body. The beast ferociously attacked every orifice of my body, and the strange discomfort reminded me of the final days of a pregnancy. Was I going to give birth to the monster or was it going to push me back out into the real world? It was probably this terrifying doubt that was most responsible for burning me out and keeping me from understanding the incessant muttering going on in my brain.

"You get better by doing what you like," old Dr. Bernard insisted, on the other end of the phone line for the hundredth time.

Unable to add two plus two correctly, I spent my days dying like grass in the summer. I was calmly slipping away, disconnected from my own flesh. Then, once the internal buzzing stopped, it was like an immense exhaustion, heavy as winter, came and laid down in my veins.

I was almost forty years old and I'd never stopped to think about my own needs or what could make me happy; that was why it was taking so long to get better. The children were trying to spoil me; even if, over the years, they'd learned to get along without me. They brought me tea, where I was lying in a lounge chair outside, in front of the house. I had an urgent need for space. My eyes hurt as, wide-open, they struggled to make out something that was worthwhile. I spent hours watching the show put on by the leaves as they fell from the big maple tree. Heavy with colour, I watched them spin, dance, and then land on the grass, on the little white table near my chair, or even occasionally in my half-full cup. It was their dying moment that finally managed to touch me: bright vermillion and dancing their way to the ground... red as love or the little raspberries Dad used to love.

I suddenly felt like getting up and walking towards that magnificent colour, blazing with emotion. Peacefully, I started to think that perhaps writing would make me feel better and make me happier.

In April, I told Mr. Dimitri I wouldn't be coming back to work. Leaving the business meant taking a financial loss, because, since he didn't agree with my decision, he refused to pay me my share of the profits. Too weak to argue, I signed all the papers.

One day, a regular customer called me at home to encourage me a bit. A textile magnate, he claimed I would soon be better and offered to take me out to dinner just so I could get out of the house occasionally.

It took a long time for me to heal. Sometimes, I would spend the whole day asleep on the sofa. Then, peacefully, I decided to stop trying to figure out what was happening to me; I let go and finally found the strength to concentrate on what would really make me happy.

When summer again turned to fall, I got into the habit of having coffee in a big restaurant near Rosemère bridge; it was called the *Restaurant Sainte-Rose*. Slowly, with my head hidden between two stacks of dishes, I began to write in my journal. The pen would shyly scratch along the bluish lines of the spiral notebook. It helped pass the time and I noticed that little by little the monster was releasing the terrible grip it had on my soul.

Every morning, I arrived when the two stars disappeared from the sky and I would see hundreds of dreams – some timid, others more confident – rising from between the lines in the notebook. I could make out grandfathers with fabulous promises, unbeatable mothers, fishermen soaked to the skin, poets sitting on huge birds, and even an occasional Micmac killing a Huron enemy; I could see radiant actresses bowing before they slipped behind the curtain; and lively fish swimming along country streams. Every day I stepped into a new castle built from words and discovered how the millions of elements that make up writing can warm you when you're close to them. I would find myself laughing at the show put on by the letters as they leapt across the snowy pages of my notebook. I would make an effort to use words that brought something to the page without attacking it, and I had a special appreciation for expressions with the magnificent power to draw pictures.

When life again filled me with an entanglement of hellish vines, I felt the need to express the overwhelming despair, and wrote about the strangling feeling it caused in me. Instead of leaving a trail of white stones, like the little child wandering in the woods, I wrote so that I could find a path that would lead back to myself. Writing also allowed me to realize that a garden of diamonds still existed in my imaginary heaven. Little by little, with each fragile step, my soul came back to life, like a newborn, stretching his arms and legs one by one.

As I wrote, the *Restaurant Sainte-Rose* became like a beautiful female character, and seemed like the guardian angel of a small section of the Ile-Jésus, between Fabreville and Auteuil. Mother Rose protected her town, where the main businesses were clothing stores and antique shops, crammed in around the church and the Dragon hardware store. I consumed several cups of coffee daily as I confided all my thoughts in the notebooks. I felt like I was dreaming: I would finish one story just where I would begin another and I was getting better without even realising it. It often seemed like lifting a page from the notebook would reveal a web of roots stretching between the writing and my heart.

Finally, after five long months of writing therapy, my vital arteries were completely unblocked. The preposterous evil characters gave way to a study of the restaurant's real customers. I would also note each activity linked to the restaurant business as if one day my life would depend on the accuracy of my descriptions.

My life would indeed one day depend on that accuracy, but I was still far from realizing that this was filtering into me; and equally far from recognizing that, as I invented lives for real characters that I didn't know, what I was doing was recreating my own life through the sublime vocation of writing.

As I recovered, the words began to flow out of me onto the page so quickly I couldn't keep up with them. I could no longer silence my childhood in Gaspésie, my mother's illness, Donnacona, my classical studies, my Greek adventure, the big Greek restaurant, and the tragedy of my burnout. Then, one fine morning, although I hadn't run out of black ink or white pages to write on, I found myself leafing through the want ads in the newspaper.

I then understood that I'd gotten everything out of my system and that the therapy had been successful. The patient could finally move on to something else.

Suffering comes from the fact that we don't always understand what's happening to us. We have no idea how fate can force our lives into a 180-degree turn. In my case, an angel named Rose organized everything for me from her lighthouse near the bridge. To point me in the right direction, as I rebuilt a life in the notebooks, the angel focused my attention on my illness and then used a fork to draw a breakfast plate in my heart.

CHAPTER 10

Registering the Name

ON THAT MAY MORNING IN 1987, THE LINE AT THE MONTREAL Court Building's registration department was already long. A row of Asians, Italians, Greeks, and a few blond heads were waiting along the low wall leading to the window where a wizened civil servant was baptising Quebec's business-minded citizens' first steps. I joined the parade, just behind a young version of Yoko Ono, with a red mane and dark glasses, who was dragging her precious life around in a huge black metal briefcase that hammered against the floor each time the line advanced after another candidate made it to the window.

My business wasn't so impressive; it fit on a notebook page where I'd scribbled a few possibilities of homage to my new Sainte-Rose confidante: *Les petits matins de Rose, Chez Rose, Déjeuners chez Rose, Rose-Cocos, Rose-Omelettes*. Because the imaginary character had allowed my rebirth to take place under her roof, I wanted to include her in the name of the little restaurant that had imposed itself upon me a short while before.

Miss Côte-Vertu was the name of a snack bar on a street corner in a little city that had hatched within the big city of Montreal. When I'd stepped into the abandoned little place, I'd immediately been attracted to the wide body of the counter, as if I'd had an advance glimpse of the whole place bustling with customers at each table. I'd found the twenty-nine seat restaurant one morning when I was driving my son to his job during a transit strike. I have a very precise memory of the surprise I felt when I saw the sign "RESTAURANT FOR SALE." We'd been driving along Côte-Vertu Street every morning for more than a week without noticing it. As soon as I read those three words, I knew that the year I'd spent wandering would end there, in that restaurant I would make my own. After I dropped off my son, I went back to the parking lot at 605 Côte-Vertu, where, miraculously, there was a phone booth. I dialled the number that appeared at the bottom of the sign.

Thirteen days later, there I was, waiting in a government office to register the name of my business. In my head, a little voice had whispered that I should buy the snack bar, clean it up, paint it, and use it to feed my children. And I had felt that the place would provide me with an infinite number of stories to write, in my free time, at home, as I stirred my soups.

I was still hesitating between *Rose-Cocos* and *Rose-Omelette* when the little Asian woman in front of me energetically closed her briefcase. From behind his window, the civil servant informed me that all the names with Rose I was proposing had already been taken and he suggested that, before I choose a name, I should check the municipal files where all the ones that were already in use were registered. Behind me, the line was still as long as when I'd arrived, and that meant I'd have to wait several more hours. As I stood there grumbling, the civil servant opened the little door in his window and asked me my name. I answered him. After a few keystrokes, he happily said, "*Chez Cora*: never been used! Call it *Chez Cora* or *Omelettes Cora*, if you don't want to wait anymore. Otherwise, get back in line. Next!"

In a fraction of a second, I thought of all the hours I'd spent *chez Rose*. Then, strangely, I also thought of Grandma Cora who'd had a restaurant of her own, too. The name could refer to her.

I'd been out of work for a year. The magazine *La Vie en rose* had refused my application to be a free-lance writer, the Château Champlain wasn't interested in hiring me as a hostess, and Dalmy's Canada didn't want me as a store manager. My house was for sale and I needed to start making a salary as soon as possible. *Chez Cora* or *Chez Margot*, I really didn't have any time to waste. It was already after noon and I had a meeting at two with the seller's attorney. I had to move fast. I'd explain destiny's little trick to Rose later.

"Next!" repeated the civil servant, impatiently.

"Wait, wait! I'll take it. I'll take the *Chez Cora* that's never been used."

"Give me the name and complete address of the business, please."

And that's how I became the owner of *Chez Cora*, 605 Côte-Vertu Street, in Saint-Laurent.

The place was going to become my home. Still, I'd never thought that one day my name would appear on a commercial sign. On the other hand, I had a very clear vision of the rest of it, and that is what I explained to the sign maker.

"I want a big yellow sun, and a little coffee cup at the bottom, next to the address."

"Okay! We can make that for you out of a big sheet of wood, three colours on a white background, for six hundred and thirty five dollars."

"That's awfully expensive!"

"It's because we'll have to cut out the rays of the sun. Is that okay with you, ma'am?"

"At that price, I hope installation is included."

"Cutting out detailed shapes is hard and always very expensive, little lady."

"If you say so! Okay. I'll pay you in three weeks, but I need the sign by next Monday."

"Okay! I suppose I can trust a mother with three children...You'll have it for Monday."

"Including installation, don't forget."

"Yeah, well, I guess we have to give old *Miss Côte-Vertu* a chance to get herself a good make-over."

CHAPTER 11

Selling the Family House

LUCKILY, AFTER A PAINSTAKING INSPECTION, THE SON OF A civil servant opted to purchase our white house on Chamberlain Street in Boisbriand; the very one I'd seen melt and dissolve into a blanket of asphalt so many times when I was writing. The house had been carefully examined a thousand times following the declaration of my impending inability to pay the mortgage. The former owner, Mr. Montplaisir, had moved out after he'd won two million dollars in the lottery. Now, it had been over a year since I'd left my job and I was spending my days writing in a restaurant in Sainte-Rose, between the classified ads in *La Presse*, the flecked sofa in the living room, and the turquoise dreams I always used to drown any vulgar material worry I might have.

The civil servant preceded his son through the door, and went right up into the attic, where he'd even gone during his first visit to the house. They examined all the pipes, ceilings, floors, incoming plumbing, and outgoing ventilation. The way the plugs were arranged seemed to be of the utmost importance to the son, a letter carrier by trade. The attentive son was shorter than his father, and torn between working for the city and his beautiful, heavy mother who smelled like herbs and was wearing a pure-wool knit jacket. A mother who was already thinking of her future grandchildren playing in the fenced-in yard, and who would certainly not be in danger of getting hit by a car on their bikes in the Chamberlain Street development, where you could still hear the cows mooing at milking time.

A week after their first invasion, the whole clan agreed to purchase the house. One fine Tuesday, the civil servant, in his Sunday best, showed up with all his pride and insisted on inspecting the property one last time.

"Hmpf! To check a few details."

And to please his daughter-in-law Jacqueline, whom I was meeting for the first time. She stood behind her mother-in-law in cute little red plastic boots, wearing the season's first straw hat on her head.

"A good country girl," the matriarch of the clan hurried to tell me, once she'd introduced us. "Jacqui's a girl from back home in Abitibi; she knows how to sew anything a woman could want!"

From the moment she came in, Jacqueline looked at me intently. Her eyes moved rapidly and she seemed to be taking pictures of everything around me: the old quilt, my notebook, the reproduction of the *Ravishment of Psyche* hanging over the blue rattan table, Saturday's edition of *La Presse*, the apple-shaped tea cup, the open books lying everywhere and the fat cat who was staring right back at her.

Twice her father-in-law called to her from the basement, but she remained motionless in the washable Orlan cape her mother-in-law had probably knit for her.

"Jacqui! Come here and I'll tell you about the storage," he yelled again from the depths of the cellar.

The poor girl headed for the stairs like a depressed bird.

Odette later apologized for Jacqui's rudeness, commenting that the way she stared at strangers made no sense.

"She and her Home Ec education are straight out of the country. Jacqueline was second in her class and the daughter of a municipal councillor; those things are important when you're thinking about the future of your grandchildren."

Odette didn't stop talking until her husband came back upstairs with Jacqueline and his son. The chief requested permission to sit down and the whole tribe invaded the two loveseats opposite me.

"I'm thinking," the *pater familias* stated ceremoniously.

He closed his eyes and, through the little folds of

skin, I could see him calculating the price, adding the advantages and subtracting the costs. I watched his thin face bounce back and forth between approval and doubt. A doubt that was big enough to make the civil servant's brain swell as he sank into the soft belly of the loveseat. Everyone was quiet. Without a sound, the cat climbed onto my shoulder; he too wanted to hear what the opening lips of the father were about to let loose.

"When would you be moving out?"

In my head, I was already gone; I'd been strolling along interminable rows of duplexes, looking for a place to live that would cost less than three hundred dollars a month and shelter half the belongings of the gypsy family we were about to become. I'd already given everything we didn't need any more to charity. The money from selling the house would go toward finalizing the purchase of the snack bar. That was the only important thing. I had to buy paint, construction supplies for the renovation, new chairs, nice flowered fabric for the curtains and tablecloths, and replacement dishware; the sign was going to cost $625, and I'd also have to pay the lawyer; the rest would pay for the first order of food I needed for the opening.

Suddenly, a serious "Yes" coming from the letter carrier's mouth brought me right back to the living room in Boisbriand, where the father and son together said "Yes" again, as if they were looking for indispensible female agreement. The double "yes" rolled around the living room, jumping from one chair to the next. It fell onto the cover of my notebook, enthusiastically, politely and, finally, extremely embarrassed.

So I hurriedly replied, "Yes! We'll be out as soon as possible, so Jacqueline has time to plant those big Abitibi vegetables in the garden!"

CHAPTER 12

The First Restaurant

At 605 Côte-Vertu Street, work went on in an enthusiastic atmosphere. I sewed curtains and pretty tablecloths in the same flowered fabric. I covered the walls in a white faux plaster finish while my children painted the pipes and fan blades in a beautiful contrasting black. We bought new metal chairs with black leatherette backs and an old cash register that we set up in front, at the end of the counter. On the little tables behind the till, we placed Titan's radio and all the dishware we still had from late Grandma Joséphine's service.

"It will remind us of our country roots," declared my daughter Julia.

"We'll put big jars of jam on display like the ones in the well-stocked pantries in the houses in Gaspésie," I quickly added.

Julia put two big soup spoons in a metal canning

ring. Marie, Titan's girlfriend, suggested that we put a cruet of homemade syrup on each table. Ultimately, we put together quite a collection of syrup containers. All of them were different because they, like the dishes, had been found in different places: second hand stores, flea markets, and liquidation centers, which were already getting popular back then.

The restaurant business I was about to get into was completely different than what I had been doing prior to falling ill; in the big deli, no one knew how much the cups cost because they came straight from China in lots of twenty-five cases. We never worried about the little details; or about the unevenly cut pieces of pastry that would end up in the garbage; or about the many pieces of cutlery that would disappear after they were wrapped up in the big, soiled placemats with the cigarette butts from the emptied ash trays; or about the manager's unusual sadness; or about employees who cried, gossiped, said nothing, or moved on.

Thank God, I'd already learned that the originality of a concept might be able to bring success, but that it doesn't guarantee a long life. And I already understood that, when you lower your prices to attract or keep customers, you end up losing them despite it all, because there will always be someone crazier or more desperate than you who will drop their prices even more.

***

Since we'd taken over, the former *Miss Côte-Vertu* had been completely transformed. She was opening her arms in welcome after being closed for three long years. Certainly, over the course of the last two years, she'd undergone several attempts to bring her back to life. We were told that an Arab man had swathed her in red velvet and sold *shish taouk* for eighty-two days; someone else had covered her walls in synthetic leather in the hopes of attracting a few rare night owls with laser discs. For her last metamorphosis, the one that confirmed she was really dead once and for all, her veins had been stuffed with so much electrical current that, two hours after the official opening of *Les Fondues de la Princesse*, she had a brilliant meltdown, and took three bubble gum pink window valences from the Linen Chest and a still-unpaid lease deposit with her. Not to mention the court battle that went on for four months.

Miss Côte-Vertu's regulars had mourned her for a long time. Disappointed and inconsolable, they each held, deep in their hearts, a particular event she'd been involved with: a relationship, a promise, a painful break-up.

The greasy spoon had had its hour of glory back when its Greek owner staggered back and forth between the cash register and clanking pots, watching over his wife, his daughter, and the buxom waitress Manon, who alone assured that the Hellenic establishment made a profit. In those days, the Greek owner cooked his continental menu every morning while cursing the planet Earth. He begged the heavens to be lenient with his ventilation, he begged his wife to put less meat in each portion of London steak, and he begged Adrianna, his beloved daughter and vessel of the family's higher education, to tell him the best ways to get rich. He figured there must be a way to get rich without investing too much, in Canadian trains or real estate, in gold bricks, or in the American secrets that schools taught to people like his daughter who knew how to read and write.

Even after he'd finally purchased the building after fifteen years of loyal service at the stove, Angelo Machinpoulos remained convinced that there were other ways of doing things and eventually abandoned the little restaurant that had made him almost rich, asthmatic, and more miserable than all the emaciated hills of his homeland.

CHAPTER 13

The "Bonjour" Breakfast

The old regulars, attracted by the large sun that had appeared on *Miss Côte-Vertu's* cheek, were the first ones to come through the door of *Chez Cora*. The big yellow rays coming from the wooden sign and the two roosters with red lacquer combs informed them they'd be welcomed "as soon as the sun rises from its bluish eiderdown." Shyly they came in, examining each of the establishment's strange new decorations.

"*Miss Côte-Vertu* has been reborn," the bravest ones would say. "She's pleasant and welcoming, like fresh, warm dew, white and voluptuous with big, new, white cups that have wide handles for the cement workers' thumbs."

"*Miss Côte-Vertu* is more beautiful than ever!" others would daringly add.

She was more attractive, but her beauty was different; there was something nostalgic about her, because as soon as you stepped inside, you felt like one of your great-aunts was going to appear at the stove or like your own grandmother was going to come serve your omelette. *Miss Côte-Vertu* really had changed: she'd gone from being a flattered floozy to a warm mother!

Despite Machinpoulos's warnings – he thought I looked like an old nun, that I wasn't sexy enough, and didn't know enough about marketing – I continued to button my jacket up to my neck and play the role of the mother hen. Marie, who was now working at my side as a waitress, could do nothing but agree with me, though she'd subtly raise her skirt to show off the legs of a young chick.

The people who worked at Canadair came in first; at 6:10 or 6:15, they'd start arriving with the Marchand Électrique employees and the others who worked in the factories on Pelletier Street. City police officers and firefighters showed up on the fourth day with a few construction workers from the company that was putting up buildings on Montpellier Street.

"*Bonjour*!" Marie said politely.

"Two eggs with bacon!" replied a cheeky man covered in dried cement.

"*Bonjour*!" Marie insisted.

"Two eggs with bacon!" replied the electrician.

"Okay! Sunny side up or over?"

"Sunny side up. Do you have fried potatoes to go with that?" asked the triumphant fellow.

Oh, yes, we sure did have some wonderful fried

potatoes, like the ones my father used to make us on Saturday with the left over boiled potatoes from the week.

"Boss, one BONJOUR, sunny side up," Marie shouted to me. "Because when I say '*bonjour*,'" she added, "they answer, 'Two eggs with bacon.'"

This was indeed the kind of morning greeting the Greek owner used to serve his faithful customers: two eggs with bacon, ham or sausage, crêpes from a mix, or three half slices of bread dunked in beaten eggs and fried in the pan that had been used to make the previous night's filet of sole. Not surprising that the buxom Manon's charms were required to help build up the customers' appetite.

Since we didn't have anything that resembled that particular prized profile, we quickly had to turn to other means of seduction, which eventually turned out to be more efficient and longer lasting. We charmed customers with big spoonfuls of real homemade syrup that we'd add a couple of drops of vanilla to in order to sweeten it; we surprised them by cooking succulent *cretons* [3] whose wonderful aroma always made you have to taste them; and we brought back the real crêpe batter that our grandmothers used to pour into their big black cast-iron pans. I remembered well the white flour mixture that my mother used to make herself in the kitchen in Caplan, to which she would add large eggs, one by one, into the folds of the batter.

Jehane Benoit's cooking encyclopedia quickly

[3] slow cooked, shredded pork

replaced *The Cinderella Complex* on my pillow. *La Cuisine raisonnée* and *Cuisine des belles fermières* became my favourite reading material. I'd often fall asleep with an illustration of poor man's pudding or a pineapple upside-down cake stuck to my forehead. It was easy for me to learn by reading; but I realized it would be difficult for me to write with the hustle and bustle of the daily routine. In fact, it turned out to be impossible. I didn't write another line after for ten years after the snack bar opened, except for an occasional short story about a giant stretched out from one end of the restaurant to the other, with his toes in the entryway and his head on the back balcony. But the fictional giant was soon forgotten so all the space and energy could be devoted to the customers, who were becoming more and more numerous. They were coming to us with their own stories, which Marie and I had to stock in our heads so that, when we were leaning on the counter, we could answer them like they were real family.

CHAPTER 14

The Bobby Button Breakfast

Bobby Button was one of the first customers whose personality became imprinted on my memory. Because Bobby had the unpleasant habit of never forgetting the little silver spoon he had with him when he came out of his mother's womb. Spoiled as he was, he would have turned up his nose at her milk if it had been socially acceptable.

Bobby was introduced to *Chez Cora* by the button designer in his family's clothing factory. Bobby absolutely loved our food, but he was always the one who ended up with the little stone in Friday's pea soup, or a miniscule drop of blood on the crinoline of his egg, or, worst of all, a real *homo sapiens* hair, which would cause him to leap up from his chair to indignantly pull the vile thing from his mouth in front of everyone.

Whenever he stopped by, Bobby always demanded a special breakfast: a Bonjour, with ham instead of bacon; or a bacon crêpe without the cheddar it was usually served with, or with camembert or brie instead of cheddar.

"Mom, guess what Bobby wants this morning!" Julia said to me one morning, looking dismayed.

"Go on, Julia, let me hear your order; we'll make him what he wants."

"Bobby wants a bacon omelette with tomatoes..."

"Okay, that's easy!"

"Wait, Mom! Bobby wants you to serve his omelette with two big white flour crêpes!"

I was already thanking the heavens for having sent him to us when that pretentious young man popped his head into my kitchen.

"Bobby, an omelette between two big crêpes is a great idea. I never would have thought of it myself!"

After I'd hidden the omelette between the two big crêpes, I had to cut the thick sandwich in four pieces before I could place it in the oblong dish we served the crêpes in. And then it suddenly looked like a big, flat club sandwich. A mountain of fruit to replace the fries and it was perfect! I was delighted. Thanks to my demanding customer, the BOBBY BUTTON MORNING CLUB had just been added to the list of signature dishes at *Chez Cora's*.

CHAPTER 15

The Jo Tabah Breakfast

As a manufacturer of work uniforms, like Bobby Button, Jo Tabah also earned his living attracting the inhabitants of busy Chabanel Street. When he ventured for the first time into the newly redecorated snack bar where he'd once been a regular, he still had to lower his head to come through the door and reel in his legs to get them to fit under the tiny table for two. Then, inhaling the aroma coming from the coffee pot, he gave the waitress his order.

"Two eggs sunny side up, and two sausages, too, Miss."

"One Bonjour, with two sausages!" Marie shouts to me.

"No, Miss. All I want is two eggs sunny side up with bacon, and two sausages."

Marie was trying to explain that "two eggs with bacon" was now called a Bonjour in our restaurant when the gentleman launched into his own explanation for her.

"One JO TABAH, sunny side up!" Marie finally concluded, directing her personal loudspeaker towards my ear.

Deadly serious, Jo Tabah drank three cups of coffee before the plate had time to land in front of him. He poured a generous amount of ketchup over his eggs and swallowed them down without blinking, paid for his breakfast and left Marie a generous tip.

Jo Tabah proved he was worthy of the honour we had bestowed upon him by becoming a regular at *Chez Cora's*. He returned every other day that Allah placed at his apron-cutter's feet.

CHAPTER 16

Every Customer is a Personality

THE SAINT-JOACHIM CLAN LIVED SPREAD OUT AROUND A bunker built from real Italian marble, located relatively close to the snack bar. In this family of sad-souled boys, the youngest, Fafard, a mechanic, appeared to have been part of the furnishings we purchased with the restaurant. Twenty times a day, we would catch him pretending to read something important in the newspaper. He had the odd habit of polishing the spoon for his coffee, which never seemed to be clean enough for him and he grumbled about the thickness of his crêpe while he ate it. Fafard was a big blowhard when it came to talking about life, and especially about sex, which is where he directed his romantic disappointment. We were told that he had been betrayed by his best friend, in his own bed, while he was working overtime so he could buy the ruby his fiancée wanted. Ever since that betrayel, Fafard got his revenge by provoking people; when he talked about sex everything he said was both assertive and incoherent. Of course, because he'd been coming to the snack bar ever since he'd become an experienced adult, he'd known Manon, as well as all of the old restaurant's regular customers.

His big brother Marcel was also a constant customer and a mechanic. He knew the address of every pretty girl in the town and every one of the ailing motors in its parking lots. Marcel was much quieter than his brother, and when he spoke, he rarely went so far as to use a complete sentence. It always seemed like the only thing he was ever interested in was bringing old Corvettes back to life. Marcel lived with another brother, a seller of second-hand goods and old three-legged chairs, who was too poor to come to us for an eighty cent cup of coffee. This brother, Emile, came through our door just once, the day the Saint-Joachim boys' father died. It was the fourth brother, Bertrand, a carpet cleaner who'd married outside the clan, who paid for the multitude of coffees the boys consumed that day, man to man, without shedding a single tear.

Our friend Fafard never mentioned his mother, not even when Marie would sit down next to him for a "heart to heart," as she liked to say. Sometimes, around eleven o'clock, after the breakfast dishes were done and when the aroma of dessert was struggling to escape from the oven, the young man would manage to whisper a few secrets to the nice waitress. He talked about his job, his bosses, the people he worked with, the increase in minimum wage he couldn't care less about because it didn't erase the risk of having a big piece of equipment squash one of your arms or your feet. For Marie, he described the people he worked with and the many frustrations the capitalist system imposed on the working class.

CHAPTER 17

Breakfast as our Specialty

I STILL HADN'T WRITTEN A SINGLE LINE AND EVERY DAY I HAD to get up before dawn, put on the bleached white apron my job required, braid my hair and wake up poor Marie (who was then living with me and always complained about not having enough time to finish her dream). She'd come to *Chez Cora* with her hair still a mess, sometimes with holes in her stockings, and, most of the time, in a skirt that was too tight – and that she'd put on backwards!

"Two steps away from happiness," Maurice, the nice Délipro delivery man would exclaim.

The indefinable quibbling, full of love and reproaches, that was always going on between Marie and me, in public and in private, contributed greatly to our popularity. The way we interacted had an effect on everyone who came into the snack bar. I criticized her soup for being too thick, she criticized the bacon I hadn't cooked enough; we discussed the needless spending of money on Windex. And the way she talked so surprisingly casually to the customers, from the youngest to the oldest! To tell the truth, I was jealous of the warm familiarity that allowed her to immediately have a connection with every soul who crossed her path. I wanted to be part of that camaraderie with everyone, to stop feeling so strangely different and jump right into the crowd, like a groundhog jumping into its square of earth.

Ironically, the firefighters were often the ones who lit the fires at the snack bar: the blessed fire for the coffee, the one for the grill where we made the eggs, and the one on the Garland gas stove for the first load of fried potatoes. The lads arrived even before we did and they got into the habit of helping us start the day as they hummed a happy tune, confirming things were going well for them.

One particularly busy Friday, about four months after we opened, a strange man came and set arms as wide as paddles down on the counter next to the kitchen. We'd just finished the breakfast dishes when the stranger leaned so far forward he could almost touch the old equipment we'd purchased from Machinpoulos. Then, like any other new customer, he asked about our background. He thought for a moment, and, as he stared right at me, asked how long we planned to continue working with our old metal antiques.

The stranger was right to ask us. Our kitchen was

full of all kinds of old-fashioned equipment that was used to prepare what every snack bar on the planet (at least my planet!) served its clientele in 1980: club sandwiches that got smashed when they were cut, hot-dogs whose innards were soggy and disgusting, hamburgers that were charred because the wood stove didn't work correctly, and poutine with canned gravy that even my own children wouldn't eat! When this man, a skilled second-hand goods salesman, offered to replace our fryer, grill, stove, and steamer with a large cooktop that came from a construction site near James Bay, for the modest sum of five hundred dollars, I felt like he had read my mind.

Since breakfast was always our most popular meal, I decided at that very moment to shift the restaurant's focus to breakfast.

"Okay, I accept. We'll go to Saint-Hyacinthe tonight to see your cooktop, with, uh, three hundred dollars."

"It's a deal, ma'am. You won't have any regrets about your decision."

We never did regret it. I'd bought the snack bar in order to earn a living, and here, after just a few months of hard work I had, a marvellous idea, inspired by a man who sold second-hand goods.

I would realize later that Providence always lets us take our first steps before it shows itself. It waits for us to show that we're really engaged in the choices we've made, and when it sees we've jumped in with both feet, it gives us a little tap with its magic wand. No, no, it doesn't come and sit on our living room sofa to talk about the future: it waits till we start to get our hands dirty.

In my case, Providence had allowed me to answer the call of my vocation with my own free will — choosing to work, get my hands dirty, buy the snack bar where I'd invested my whole nest egg, slave away to renovate it, and put all my energy into serving its clientele.

Then, when it was sure I was serious, in a fraction of a second, it changed my life by shifting the focus of the little restaurant. I soon discovered that it had also injected into my veins the courage and personality I'd need to fulfill my new mission.

That's how I ended up sometimes with up to ten sets of eggs sizzling on my used Miraclean cooktop. I had to move fast to be sure the first ones on the grill bid *au revoir* to their neighbours and stepped out of line before the heat dried them out. Each set of eggs was the object of a particular order: over, sunny side up, well done, or runny. The sizzling dancers let the big metal spatula scoop them up and set them down on the white plate, next to crescent-shaped slices of ham or between two thick savoury sausages.

My hands kept busy over the mob of yellow heads and my ears, instead of hearing the sizzling of the eggs on the hot surface, began to notice a phenomenon. I realized I wasn't alone in the kitchen. Since the big cooktop had been installed, a translucent hand had been fluttering above my own. All-seeing eyes occupied the space next to my own, endowed with powers of analysis that allowed them to envisage all sorts of fantastic possibilities. Even my voice, I often noticed, was passing through a sieve and coming out creamier, clearer, and going deeper into my customers' hearts. My body became stronger, as if it had been miraculously remade. I was able to work ten or twelve hours straight without feeling tired and without feeling the burning sensation that occurs in feet that can't hold up under the body's weight anymore. From time to time, the transparent angel would also take over my head. It completely rejuvenated my imagination, giving it the ability to invent new stories where taste and presentation were the heroes. Although I was too stubborn certain days to believe it existed, Providence showed up again and again. Sometimes it came in through a crack in a window, or settled onto a crêpe, or spoke in soft words just as I was about to lose faith.

CHAPTER 18

An Apple Crêpe for the Baker

SOMETIMES, PROVIDENCE WOULD SHOW ITSELF TO ME BY sending angels. For example, every morning, Mr. Pom, the man who delivered our bread, gave us the opportunity to be part of his happy universe. Between jokes, he would line up his loaves of bread behind our counter as he swung his huge body back and forth. When he was done, he'd have a cup or two of coffee.

"When it smells good, it tastes even better."

Quite often, we would create a new dish just for him so we could have the pleasure of watching him lick his chops. One day in October it was the delicious apple crêpe that was a regular item on our menu for years. We spread the crêpe batter on the cooktop with a thin wooden stick, then let it cook through before we turned it over. On the side of the crêpe that was already browned, we grated almost a whole large red apple. We covered the layer of fruit with grated, extra old cheddar cheese, then sprinkled it with cinnamon. Then we folded the crêpe in half and let cook a few minutes more so that the cheese melted through the layer of fruit.

Every time we served this masterpiece to the baker, his eyes would be as wide as saucers. But we could never forget to place the salt shaker full of cinnamon within his reach on the counter, because he would always add more, stating that things didn't taste the way they used to. And he knew about the taste of food since he was the one who made the family spaghetti sauce every Saturday, being sure to add enough pepper, Italian spices, and Bovril, while Mrs. Pom did volunteer work, personally washing the eighteen residents at *Les Près verts*, a nursing home in Lachine.

Probably fearing such exile, 88-year-old Mr. Sarto happily climbed the two cement steps in front of the snack bar and then went and sat by his friend the blowhard Fafard. Then, as if to block the trembling such an effort caused in his bones, he'd quickly clasp his tiny hands, hiding them under the counter. Mr. Sarto ordered very sweet tea and waited for his friend to say something saucy that would likely get under his skin. Marie didn't really like the old man and never missed the chance to scrape his fingers when she was cleaning the counter with a solution of bleach and water — sometimes she would even wait until he was all settled in before she'd start cleaning. She'd scrub the orange surface of the counter until the old fellow couldn't breathe. Then he'd turn around, half pale, half green, laugh at Fafard and fall onto the snake-shaped handle of his cane. He'd cough, toss a dime to the waitress and disappear till the next day.

"Now we can take the cake out of the oven!" Marie would shout. "The old crow's gone."

Marie was referring to the dessert I made every day. In a big pan, I'd put a layer of sugar and several rows of sliced fresh fruit (apples, pears, peaches, and occasionally cherries when they were in season), and sprinkle a layer of nutmeg or vanilla, depending on the fruit. Then I'd cover the whole mixture with a cake batter, one of *Chatelaine* magazine's favourite recipes. This upside-down cake knocked everyone off their feet and some days at lunch time there were men in dark suits fighting over the last pieces. Covered with real whipped cream, like no other snack bar was serving, even back then, the dessert spoke directly to the heart of the customer, with the same words once used by his grandmother Béatrice, Marie-Ange, or Georgina, when she used to take the time to cook and prepare dishes delicious enough to be worthy of her ancestors.

Our customers probably appreciated our food because when they ate our soup, or dessert, or shepherd's pie, they felt like they were part of something larger than their current reality. It was like *Chez Cora* was a huge movie screen and they had the starring roles in the film. Despite the ups and downs of my imagination, it seemed that my cooking was continuing a certain tradition — I felt that the taste of what we served brought to life the memory of a past where our customers wished they still lived. I was also beginning to think that our profession wasn't only about food, but also about delighting people. We produced for them the wonderful childhood pleasure of a big spoonful of tasty goodness slipping into their mouths. We were there to take our customers back in time, and help them believe once again that life was fun, tasty and invigorating.

CHAPTER 19

The ROSEMARY'S SUNDAY Breakfast

THOUGH WE HADN'T RECEIVED PERMISSION TO SERVE MEALS outside, we took a chance and set up four small tables in the narrow space between the restaurant's front window and the street. The heat inside the restaurant resulted in many customers seeking out these few seats.

My daughter Julia wasn't the fastest waitress we had, but she was the one who brought in the most customers. Working on the new outside terrace, she had to be good at maintaining peace among the customers as they fought over the chairs. So, on one particularly hot Sunday, she didn't have time to chat with the English-speaking woman who asked her for a BONJOUR (two eggs with bacon) "with two small crêpes with blueberries on the same plate, please."

"No problem! Would you tell me your name?"

"Why? Why should I tell you my name just to get breakfast?"

"Don't worry, it's just because of my mother. She has a knack for inventing names for new breakfasts."

"My name is Rosemary Martingale," replied the customer, reassured.

"Mom! Mom!" shouted Julia as she came inside. "There's a Rosemary outside who wants a BONJOUR with two blueberry crêpes on the same plate."

I was going to settle for saying, "Okay, Julia," when my daughter insisted on provoking me in front of everyone.

"Mom, aren't you going to make up a name for the new dish?"

The heat put out by the new cooktop distracted me and I didn't reply. Since she hadn't gotten an answer to her question, Julia knocked two glasses against each other in front of my nose.

"Mother! The Rosemary who's outside deserves an invention."

"What are you talking about, Julia? What's *Rosemary's Baby* doing here, in this heat?"

"Not *Rosemary's Baby*, Mother, ROSEMARY'S SUNDAY!"

"What? What, Julia? What are you talking about now?"

"Mom! Let me do it, Mom! The English lady and I just invented a new dish outside. Give me a BONJOUR with two little blueberry crêpes in the same plate."

A few days later, the city ordered us to stop serving food outside. Not too disappointed, we immediately removed the tables. They had already given us an unforgettable breakfast.

CHAPTER 20

Queen Elizabeth Cake

One day, a Hydro-Québec worker brought me his grandmother's recipe for Queen Elizabeth cake, which had been copied onto fancy paper, purchased for just this purpose. The tall, sensible, polite gentleman hidden beneath the grey uniform handed me the rolled up parchment. He was a man whose eyes timidly begged for a smile, or some attention, and something about him often inspired me to give him a second bowl of soup, or to put another spoon of sauce on the hamburger steak, or warm up his coffee a third time. Because I was able to recognize a hungry look, I knew, in the bottom of my heart, that these gifts would never be enough to fill certain deep holes.

There are certain irresistible customers who bring you recipes, others send post cards from their trip to Mexico, and still others invite you to dinner just to talk! I admit that sometimes it was tough to keep strong when I was looking at a fine speciman.

So ... First chop the dates, scald them in a cup of hot water, and then let them cool off, after adding a pinch of baking soda.

In another bowl, mix white sugar, butter, and an egg, and then you pour in the creamy date batter. Then add flour to the new mixture, along with a little baking powder and a teaspoon of salt. Take the cake out of the oven and cover it with warm icing, with coconut or maybe even a few walnuts mixed in.

The next day, the handsome electrician's taste buds got a pleasant shock when he bit into my Queen Elizabeth CORA cake.

My God, how difficult it was not to be able to comfort all those kids in construction boots who would ask for real butter in the same tone of voice they'd use to tell you their most intimate experiences!

There was another client we'd nicknamed Mr. Spy because of his mysterious aura. He finally admitted to us he was Lebanese, single, broke, with no family and no attachment other than a part-time job in a pizza place. Every two weeks, with princely calm, Mr. Spy enjoyed his two eggs with sausage which, every single time, we wanted to give him free of charge. He always refused and paid his bill, leaving a generous tip and the gift of a beautiful smile, revealing so many gold teeth that Marie and I could only imagine a tragic story when we saw them.

What I probably found most painful about the

snack bar was never being able to really know my customers; never being able to really understand what their eyes were trying to tell us; never being able to really know what happened in their lives, at night, after they got home. Never knowing why they came to our place, what they found there, and why they suddenly disappeared forever. Who were they, what were they looking for, and what became of them? It was painful to have no reason to ask, to be nothing more than a fill-in mother figure who couldn't give in to the desire to create deeper relationships.

Aren't mothers passages, corridors that spirits use to make becoming flesh-and-blood a little easier? Mothers welcome, they protect, they feed and, above all, they have to facilitate their childrens' path. I discovered I liked the role of silent, complicit, anonymous confidante; I liked serving people, and doing good for others; calming the temporary suffering in an eye drowning in pain or the more tragic suffering of a finger whose wedding band had been removed. I soon realized that other people's sadness shrank as it flowed into a third ear.

CHAPTER 21

A Well-Meaning Mechanic

"YOU HAVE TO HAVE BUSINESS CARDS," MIKE SAID TO US ONE day, his tall frame proudly draped in his Esso uniform.

This brave knight of a mechanic was the husband of a strange creature whom we saw only once, on a summer afternoon. Holding her head with both hands, she told us about how she loved Mickey, about their three-room apartment on Sauvé Street and how she and her sister, Noula, saved money by running from one Jean Coutu store to another to buy facial tissue, Tide laundry detergent, and the precious ginseng Dr. Bistikiou used to prescribe for Egyptian immigrants. If he'd known she'd come to *Chez Cora*, her Mike would certainly have gotten upset with her for bothering us, for having drunk several cups of coffee, and especially for wanting to get to know us, the people her husband had been talking about constantly since *Miss Côte-Vertu's* rebirth.

Yes, some customers were starting to request business cards and Mike offered to make them for us, free of charge, at the Lebanese printing company where he worked four nights a week. He brought me cute little white cards that I gladly filled with drawings. One day, on the left side of a card, I drew a big sun with little yellow rays and wrote "Food like Mom used to make" below the name "*Chez Cora*."

"'Food like Mom used to make' is nice crêpes with syrup, shepherd's pie, macaroni with meat sauce, and chicken stew with dumplings," Marie would explain to new customers as they took their seat at the counter.

"Dum what?" the customer would ask, flabbergasted by the speed at which she spoke.

"Dumplings, sir; they're like little clouds of dough that swell up when they're cooked in bouillon."

Mr. Tony had the advantage of being the handsomest fifty-year-old man ever to come into the snack bar. He would come back occasionally to taste our famous food "like Mom used to make" and Marie eventually learned he was the happy owner of a café on Saint Laurent Street, near Jean-Talon. Marie implied that the guy really looked like he knew how to enjoy both the tropical sun and Her Majesty's head on his money.

Personally, my happiness came from drawing a little pink pig head in the *A* in *ham* on a poster, yellow bananas in the curves of the *B* in *banana cream*, and little carrots in the furrows of the *T* on a mobile proclaiming my newest cake. I decorated each word with little houses that had puffs of smoke coming from the chimneys, hard-working bees for the honey tarts, or sparkling fish swimming in the ocean of the *O* in *salmon*. I enjoyed adding flavour to the description of dishes. I loved drawing wedges of cheese, watermelon slabs, brown eggs for the omelettes, and little white chickens waltzing along the edges of big lunch plates.

***

And yes, occasionally, I would suddenly fall for the deep blue of a man's eyes. I agreed to sit with Thierry for a few hours on the grass in the park, where he'd talk for hours about his dictatorship of a marriage; a few evenings, I'd go see him skating at the arena. I liked his fantasies and the strange way his heart would look as it fought and struggled. Dreaming of going away with me, Thierry would draw cute little sailboats in ink on his placemat. But Marie was working hard to make sure the boats would never set sail, since she always threw them into the trash with the leftover real Swiss cheese omelette the love-struck fool could never finish.

"Relax, Marie! I'm not going anywhere," I'd say, to reassure her.

My only love back then was my little twenty-nine seat restaurant.

***

It's easy to be charming in a snack bar when you're willing to lean on the counter and listen: when you let men smell the cinnamon on your fingers, or watch your soft doughy cheeks as you laugh. It's easy for them to imagine cherries where your eyes should be and a wide oven door in the apron that covers your belly. They drink up your words as if they were promises made to children, and they blush when they see the little piece of fudge wrapped up just for them. I knew those gentlemen would bring me the moon, if, by any chance, I expressed the desire to brown it up on my griddle. But I didn't ask for anything. And it was exactly my silence that made them want to dive in like fish in a lake, their eyes slipping among the waves to join me, or made them want to say how much they appreciated me. In snack bars, this kind of platonic affair blossoms as quickly as tomatoes in a greenhouse.

CHAPTER 22

The Clam Chowder

The creamy chowder stock often used to stick to the bottom of Angelo's old pots. I would sweat the vegetables, adding water or milk and, when the mixture began to boil, I would thicken it with flour combined with a little water. The result was usually disastrous.

"Lumpy!" would say my youngest son Nicholas.

"Yuck! Mother! It tastes burned!" Julia would add – for once agreeing with her little brother.

The taste of stuck-on milk was the worst nightmare I had as a fledgling cook.

Then, one day, in the Saturday edition of *La Presse*, I came across the real recipe for New England clam chowder, according to the famous chef Jasper White. He lightly sautéed the clams in a pot with shallots, garlic, diced potatoes, chopped parsley and some butter. In another pot, the milk was heated (it could be diluted with a little water). When the liquid started to simmer, he thickened it with a roux made from equal parts of butter and white flour. White suggested stirring the creamy mixture gently and then pouring it into the pot of mollusks.

The following Monday, I hurried to try out the new recipe, which allowed us to serve a five-star soup at the little snack bar counter. After she had two big bowls herself, Julia insisted on practicing making the roux. At that time, we still didn't know all you had to do was keep the flour light in colour in the butter, or let it turn a darker colour, in order to get the light or dark roux the great Paul Bocuse talks about in *French Cooking*.

"Soup," my Greek brother-in-law used to say, "is the signature of a restaurant owner!"

And, just as Antigone replied to King Creon, I allowed myself to add that a client who is served bad soup should be allowed to stand up and immediately leave the establishment that served it to him. Soup, in a manner of speaking, is the hostess of the meal; it offers the first smile; warms the heart; and tells us how important the restaurant owner thinks the taste of his food is. Soup also tells us about the weather, the season, the local people's cultural habits and, almost unfailingly, about the generosity of the person who prepared it.

When a good cook is making soup, he always has to imagine twenty hungry stomachs and forty nostrils lying in wait for him on the other side of the counter. The cook shall remember that, when a customer takes a seat at the table, he still doesn't know what childhood memories will joyfully tickle his throat, and that it is this very ignorance that has the power to multiply the pleasure of eating by ten.

In a snack bar, soup also serves as a pretext to elicit all sorts of nice or funny stories about the regulars, the boss's misadventures, or simply the saint of the day. Saint Gudule, for example liked her soup with port in it. Of all the stories connected to soup, one of my favourites is the one about the "popcorn soup" that came about because an old Anglophone just didn't understand what "cream of maize" could possibly be.

CHAPTER 23

The Seventh of July

The slow Sundays of summer were a gift, since they gave me time to chat with the customers. Time, for example, to talk with Betty, the young divorcee from the building across the street.

"My husband is going to pay the rent for another four months, but then what am I going to do to make ends meet?" she asked me, since I was in a similar position, with three teenagers to feed on top of it.

"Open up a little restaurant with your friend Flora," I suggested to her. "She doesn't know what to do either, since her tennis player took off with that little blond."

"Never underestimate an Irishman!" a certain Mary E. Falcon interjected in a lively way from her seat at the counter. "The Irish are men of honour who would prefer to leave you their fortune rather than suffer disgrace," she added, nibbling a few fresh blueberries from her plate.

The Seventh of July breakfast dates back to those first summer Sundays. Since people were used to restaurants like ours being closed Sundays, those days found our little *Cora* half empty.

"We absolutely have to find a way to get the cat to taste our bowl of milk," Julia exclaimed one day, feeling distraught.

Good old Evelyne (a friend of Julia's who we had taken on as a regular waitress) suggested we lower prices on Sundays, but I answered by threatening to put an end to the time she spent with us. Finally, Fatima, the weekend helper, recommended that during the week we use the daily menu to promote the new dishes that would only be available on Sundays. We would talk about them all week long to whet our gourmands' appetites and encourage them to make the trip to see us on Sundays. We thought her suggestion was great. Now we had to come up with something that was even more exciting than everything else we'd already drawn on our walls.

"It's easy!" declared Evelyne. "Cora, what do you think?"

The wheels were already spinning around my brain. We could make our crêpes more unusual, or add some citrus zest to make the French toast better, but our customers already thought they were great dishes the way they were.

"What if we served crêpes and French toast on the same plate? What do you think, girls?" offered Evelyne.

"Okayyyy..." said Fatima, "but it needs to be more exciting."

"Not if we add a nice mountain of mixed, fresh fruit, with a sprinkling of snow," replied Julia, enthusiastically. "A sprinkling of snow" was what we called powered sugar.

I suggested that we could also serve the new dish covered in raspberry sauce and the snack bar went wild.

"Yeah! But what are we going to call this treat, boss?"

"THE EVELYNE AND FATIMA? No, it's too hard to say."

"What about today's date: *le sept de juillet*?"

"It's not very catchy," Julia remarked. "What do you think of 'THE SEVENTH OF JULY'?"

"Why not? Half our customers are Anglophones, and we'll just have to explain the name and ingredients to the other half. You can count on us," concluded Fatima, looking me in the eye.

She was exactly right. The success of the SEVENTH OF JULY we served the following Sunday was so amazing that we unanimously decided to put it on a poster on the wall the very next day, and we began to serve the dish seven days a week to our delighted customers.

CHAPTER 24

Music in the Snack Bar

WHEN SEPTEMBER CAME AROUND, FAMILIES WERE ONCE again feeling the need for a good Sunday breakfast and our complaining was suddenly replaced by an avalanche of customers. The workers had told their wives about our big apple crêpe for the bread man or the one the boss had invented for Larry Weel, the Niagara Falls cowboy. The women wanted to see these breakfasts that couldn't be explained from a distance. Personally, I was trying to understand the leap the cherubs had made: filling up our dining room Sunday after Sunday. I could see them jumping from one shoulder to another as the agile waitresses shouted their orders to me. The little white phantoms would march in step to the music and their childish antics would keep me from sinking into exhaustion.

They were all there, since I'd started making my children work weekends: Nicholas, Julia, her friend

Evelyne, and Marco, our new neighbour, whom we'd originally recruited to squeeze the three cases of oranges we needed for the customers' fresh juice.

Marco was a strange young man, floating between a modern teenager's detachment and the shadowy frustration of receiving a less-than-warm welcome into the world. He lived with his mother Madeleine on the third floor of the apartment building where we'd been neighbours since we'd sold our house in Boisbriand. The wife of an anaesthesiologist who lived somewhere else, his mother was surviving thanks to the alimony her ex's medical profession afforded her. Marco quickly learned to cover up Nicholas' shenanigans, and was very sweet and nice to us. For several weeks before his name officially appeared in the family pay book, he worked for us for free. Distracted but hardworking, he always did his job without complaining. His father the doctor couldn't believe his son could keep a job for more than four days. Nonetheless, he kept this job for several years – even after his father died of a heart attack, Marco continued to work for the CORA business.

Evelyne and Julia transformed the snack bar into a concert hall where Aretha Franklin, Janis Joplin, and some Motown groups sang louder than we chattered with the crowd of customers. The clients loved our breakfasts, the music, the mountains of fruit on slices of French toast, and the thoughtful quotes we would write every Sunday across the emptiness of the blackboard where the daily specials were usually posted.

Fatima would always choose very short, very profound statements, and she and I would read them together early in the morning, sitting on empty, overturned margarine buckets right in the middle of the kitchen. The statements were chosen at random from a little blue book we'd gotten from Overeaters Anonymous, which she and I had secretly been attending so we could learn to live better.

Despite the tiredness that came from working ten hours a day, seven days a week, despite my body's new bullet-proof vest, and despite the invisible presence of numerous angels in my life, I was still scared to death of the Last Judgment. When I was little, I'd been forced to believe in the existence of a God who was silent and questioning, and who lived very, very far away from us, up there in heaven. I was doomed to fear that awful final judgment my whole life, since it wouldn't be pronounced until I'd died, and since no one ever came back to tell us about their experiences once they'd passed on. Growing up, I'd decided that God was indeed cruel and that my salvation was at best uncertain. When we were teenagers, the priests made it a point to tell us that since we were sinners, we'd have to earn heaven by the sweat of our brow. When we insisted on learning more, the black-robed emissaries would threaten us with the worst possible punishments and invite us to be humble; with great skill, they confined us within the perfectly constructed ignorance of the religion they represented. If miracles were to continue to have the effect desired by God (or by men), it was better not to know too much and to settle for believing without understanding. That was the famous faith whose benefits we were supposed to yearn for. A faith that saved us without us having to notice it, without our being able to simply know if we were headed in the right direction. Like when you're playing Russian roulette or some other game of chance.

Stuck between my heart's best intentions and the worst manifestations of the rest of my body, I struggled along, sometimes a saint, sometimes a sinner, afflicted with that awful inability to be happy that had been handed down to us from our distant ancestors, who wanted to live like God. My soul was in pain and I searched wildly for some crack in the awful fable. I wanted to be certain that God loved me, that I was okay, good enough, devout enough, pure enough, and generous enough to deserve eternal life. To keep myself calm, and to keep on living, I searched through the waves of each new therapeutic discovery. I could be found late at night reading Bradshaw's *Inner Child*, the terrible, difficult life of Scott Peck, occasionally the Bible and even Anthony Robbins' *Unlimited Power*. My mind would roam and often felt like the head of a chicken freshly separated from its body. I was afraid, terribly afraid, that when it came to separating the wheat from the chaff, God would make an error on my account. Just like He made an error about the angel of light who revolted against Him, and just like He presumed that Mother Eve wouldn't listen to the serpent. Because that was something else they had tried to convince me of – that God really wasn't completely perfect and needed my prayers for His will to be done.

***

When she'd been faced with life's difficulties, my mother had shattered, and now it was just as hard for me as it had been for her. It really was hard to get up before dawn, waking up right in the middle of a dreamy adventure, and willingly decide to set foot in the hostile reality of the world. It was hard to smile at the broken fan; at the stinginess of Machinpoulos who was still lurking around waiting to gobble us up. Hard to think of my two younger children, who once again were left to look after themselves, and were torn by teenage preoccupations; and of my eldest Titan, who was trying to earn his daily bread as a salesman in the United States. Everything was hard for my heart, locked up under the cook's white smock. It was hard having so little money and scratching to find a bit of cash. Some days we had to scratch so deep we'd hit our souls, and shout, "Mr. Van Foutte, come back tomorrow, I don't have enough money to pay for the coffee." Or perhaps, "Maurice, come back this afternoon with the bill for the bacon." Hard, too, to ask ourselves if Machinpoulos would wait another ten days for us to pay the rent (we had purchased the business, but he still owned the building).

Of all the hundreds of recipes I was reading every night, not a single one explained the detachment that was necessary for happiness; not one succeeded in convincing me that an all-powerful, generous, and omnipotent God held a permanent place in my heart. In fact, quite the opposite occurred — all the books on personal development convinced me that God's ways were impenetrable. The gates to heaven were open to anyone searching for the divine, but paradoxically it was also easier for a camel to pass through the eye of a needle than for a rich man to cross the threshold of paradise.

Providence did everything it could to make sure my restaurant succeeded, but then God was telling me not to be too successful, not to make too much money because it was incompatible with heaven. I stubbornly tried to understand, but I never could — I arrived at the conclusion that I was condemned to this ignorance, which I still refused to describe as blissful. Sometimes, I thought the burnout I'd gone through served no purpose because I still hadn't learned to live like a normal human being, in harmony with both life's doubts and little pleasures. Yes, my energy had come back turning into a gusher inside me, but, all too often, little unsettling bubbles would still make my head spin.

I wanted desperately to know God's intentions for me. I'd been praying to Him for forty years, so His Will would be done on earth as it was in heaven, and now I was afraid that it was an achievement I wouldn't be part of. This terrible worry constantly made me feel like I didn't have enough: not enough confidence, not enough happiness, not enough hope, not enough resources, not enough talent, not enough opportunity, and not enough money. If God didn't want me, all doors closed in my heart, and even the free air I was breathing wasn't enough for me anymore.

CHAPTER 25

A Warm July

THE SECOND SUMMER ON CÔTE-VERTU GAVE ME THE opportunity to atone for all my sins. Despite the two big ceiling fans, and the two other standing fans we'd set up at each end of the counter, it was as hot as hell in the snack bar. The awful heat reminded us that wild strawberries would soon be covering the hills of Saint-Adèle. It reminded my children of picnics in the big oak tree where my father had once built a tree house just for them.

The restaurant was in a desolate state, the happiness of making people happy had died because everyone was complaining: the children, the customers, good old Marie, and even Angelo Machinpoulos, my old Greek landlord. He refused to let us cut a hole in the wall to install an air conditioner, although it still wasn't hot enough to get us to abandon ship.

"Go away if too hot; me break lease right now! Me

open this store twenty-four hours!" mumbled the old Greek, displacing as little air around him as possible.

Personally, I was putting up with it because I imagined I probably had a lot of sins to atone for. I prayed as I flipped my crêpes and I met another category of customers – those who would come no matter what, resigned to the worst.

Mrs. Georgette Edmond wore woollen beige stockings all year round, to help her arthritis. She'd been going from one snack bar to the next for twenty years looking for the cheapest cup of coffee. The first time she came to our place, in the middle of July, I gave her a cup of ours for free. In return, I received a dreadful kind of devotion all summer long, which went on through the following fall, winter, and spring, all of which I spent over the restaurant's grill. Mrs. Edmond claimed she could do me good, entertain me, she insisted. We would talk "business," about the price of eggs by the crate, the price of a bucket of margarine, and, once in a while, we'd exchange a few kind words when she'd sit near me, at the end of the counter that touched the oven. She would tell me about going to Saint-Hubert BBQ with her late husband. She would talk to me like I was her best friend, telling me about the ingenious way she'd split their half-chicken, fries, sauce, coleslaw, and roll, without attracting attention, and without ordering any unnecessary drinks that would shoot the bill into the five-dollar range, and how they'd leave the waitress a nickel, to be polite.

The Edmonds had once tasted all the pleasures life had to offer. They would go to Belmont Park once every summer. Her "Natol" hunted with a rifle. Once, in 1964, he'd even shot a bear right in the heart, a handsome brown bear that was now a rug on her bed.

Mrs. Edmond also looked after our advertising, at Jean Coutu's, Zellers, and at the medical center where they checked her blood sugar. She would tell them about how kind we were, about the free coffee and the strange story of the woman who had her children around her at the restaurant, about the colourful chickens, and about the menu weirdly written across the wall.

"I'd rather she didn't talk about me," Marie shouted at me. "I can't help it, I just can't stand her!"

Because the old witch also shared our impolite remarks, our arguments, and the jolts of love joyfully passed between the woman and her flamboyent waitress in the snack bar.

"It's unforgivable to be so real in business!" Mrs. Edmond whispered to the endocrinologist at the medical center. "Anatole Edmond, God rest his soul, never spoke to his foreman that way, in all the years he worked as a carton folder at Tucktape."

Then one day, Georgette Edmond found toast with peanut butter that was less expensive than ours at Tassos Deli, which had just opened up on Plaza Montpellier.

"Good riddance!" exclaimed Marie when our friend

Fafard told her the news. "The old chatterbox will now quit driving my boss crazy!"

***

Mike, the Lebanese mechanic, also spent the summer at *Chez Cora.* He'd come in at noon, before his shift, for a coffee and the pastry of the day. He'd take off the cap Esso required him to wear and sit right in the middle of the counter. He'd look at me and smile until I brought him the cake of the day myself. He'd chat with Gilles, a driver for Marchand Electric, about life in Quebec, about how hot it was in his country, and the price of cigarettes, which was verging on obscene. Our old friend Fafard preferred other more tempting obscenities, like the girls who strutted along the sidewalk, like cats in heat. "Because that's the way the world works!" preached the young, macho man. "Sex," he said, "is the tip of the iceberg of an incurable sickness. It's as simple as two and two make four."

"This restaurant is the best school in the world!" Nicholas would always conclude at such times.

"A much better school than Outremont High," Marie would add, turning the knife in the wound herself.

***

September's first cool winds heralded a problem that

was much more painful than the summer heat: the problem of academic education. Despite my shouting, crying, begging, and trying to convince them, each of my three children left school too early.

"They're smart, but they're too marginal," declared Mr. Perkins, the principal of Twin Oaks elementary school in 1980. "It will be almost impossible to integrate your children into the current school system."

His remark gave me the feeling that, once again, the planet was slipping away from me as it turned.

My parents were dead, my brother and my two sisters had forgotten I even existed, my ex-husband was preaching on the Parthenon in Athens, and my children were "marginal". And as for me, I was flipping crêpes to pay the bills. I'd spent thirteen months recovering from exhaustion by allowing writing to save me, and then finally, a little daily cup of coffee had shown me the direction of my new life. I'd had to show an ingenuity bordering on the miraculous in order to start a business with means as meagre as mine.

We don't always have to understand what's happening to us. I decided to trust in Providence's invisible schemes; I persevered, pressed on, closed my eyes, and moved forward like a blessed fool, settling for the sizzling of the crêpe batter as it landed on the burning griddle. There was no reason to try to understand, like the priests used to say: happy are the naive, the kingdom of heaven is theirs.

My daughter Julia was starting to master that very

same crêpe batter. She was now working full-time at *Chez Cora* and sharing Evelyne's apartment to have a bit more independence. She'd failed her last math exam and ultimately put an end to her academic worries a few days after she'd enrolled at Vanier College.

"Mom, I'll go back later, I swear to you, as soon as I figure out what so many sacrifices are good for."

I had no choice but to agree. Hadn't Mr. Dimitri told me she was an excellent barmaid? Never sick, never late. Did I have anything to hold against her? Anything besides my own frustration at having quit school to have children, at never finishing my classical studies, which I'd given up in my last year in order to have my first baby. Maybe that was what hurt me the most: the unbearable repetition of events life seemed to enjoy unleashing on one generation after the next.

Because that's how we usually imagine misery: alone, solitary, and prisoner of a hostile globe, even though it's possible to hear people suffering as they spend their nights crying in bars and their mornings in a snack bar, in the isolated motels on the edge of the city, or along Mont Royal's steep paths. Alone, we hear ourselves howl like animals, just barely humanized by despair. My way was to think about sitting at the top of the stairs that led to the snack bar basement, with the point of the big kitchen knife pressed against my chest. Mentally, I would try to imagine the best way to accidentally fall, tumbling down the stairs as the knife cut off the current within me. Unconsciously, I was looking for the best way to give up my soul while making my children think I'd sacrificed it. Because pain has its own culture: pain in childbirth, pain in learning, pain in healing, and pain in atonement. Does the moon feel pain when it trips over a cloud? Or worse yet, when it tries to make it through the night?

It would take time, many undercooked omelettes, and self-help books to get me to understand that life is perfect the way it is and that sadness is an integral part of happiness. Because, how could we describe warmth if there was no such thing as cold? How could we feel joy if we never experienced sadness? God successfully feeds the millions of birds flying over our heads every day and, poor humans that we are, we worry about not having enough oil in the salad; we suffer because we don't yet know we are perfect, complete, and divine. I myself was still very far from understanding that success, abundance and happiness were an integral part of my inheritance as a child of God.

CHAPTER 26

Jack the Alligator

JACK THE ALLIGATOR CAME INTO *CHEZ CORA* A FEW DAYS before Christmas, enticed by our buckwheat crêpe. His brothers had told him about the three big dark brown crêpes, thin and identical to the ones his mother Imelda Letellier used to cook for them on the Feast of the Assumption when they were kids, back when the world belonged to them.

The man was immediately delighted by the jar of molasses and the stick of fresh butter the waitress set down on his table, along with his first cup of coffee. Hidden away in my kitchen, I'd recognized him at once. Jack was the next-to-last son of the Letellier clan. Before getting married, I'd been his brother's girlfriend for a short time. Jack had gotten rich with Frost fences, while his wife, according to gossip, spent time in the forbidden areas of the Arab Emirates; there was an unusual love story connected to each one of Imelda's offspring. After generously buttering his pancakes, Jack rolled them up with his stout fingers. He dunked each of these handmade cigars in his molasses-filled saucer then shovelled them in, one by one, fast as a big lizard.

It was only after he'd swallowed the last mouthful that his big kiwi green eyes sought me out from among my pots and pans. Jack always had a hearty laugh and a smile was permanently affixed to his tanned face: this was his way of thanking Baby Jesus, as he called him, for the torrents of good things life showered upon him.

"Food is the only pleasure you get three times a day for your whole life!" the Alligator exclaimed, paraphrasing Talleyrand, the famous statesman. "Cora, you're even prettier now than you were back then, and even more appetizing than you were as a teenager," he added, holding my warm batter next to his heart. "Your place smells like breakfast from when I was little," he continued, in seventh heaven.

Then, forward as ever, he opened the oven door, "Hey! A real shepherd's pie!"

"With fresh, marinated beets, too," Marie added, just to torture him a little more.

Jack couldn't resist, he decided to come back for lunch. At eleven forty-five, he specifically informed us.

"Early enough to be sure I can eat all I want. Hey! And what if I asked you out to dinner while I'm at it?"

And his mother Imelda had really liked me.

"Hey! We could even stop by the retirement home

where my mother lives before dinner. What do you think, Cora?"

I didn't have a chance to answer before Jack lifted me right up off the ground; he'd just noticed the three big apple pies cooling on the shelf over the sink.

At a seafood restaurant, we enjoyed shark for dinner. We each had two big Irish coffees while we talked about Jack's previous life in the Florida Everglades, his wife, who was split between three countries, and his sons, Billy and Léo – whom I used to babysit when I was a teenager.

"We shouldn't have gotten old..." mumbled the slightly drunk Alligator. "Cora, do you remember Imelda's rhubarb pies? Hey! My little brother could eat one all by himself!"

I'll never forget Jack the Alligator's visit because the obvious delight our home cooking brought him was another clue that we were on the right track. I wasn't an accomplished chef; I'd never studied cooking and hadn't mastered a single one of the basics of the culinary arts. But I was occasionally inspired and I knew how to pull out the best from the ordinary; I had a lot of imagination and I was certain that being presented with a tasteless plate of food was the worst thing that could happen to a customer.

I had flashes of lucidity, like little suns appearing in the rest of my darkness. So many fields filled with contented alligators, astounded smiles, satisfied bellies, and intimate moments with my angels, that I often couldn't believe I was separated from God. Sometimes, He was so present within me that it felt like the rest of my life wasn't real; it was just a movie where I practiced acting like a human being. Sometimes I thought there was nothing but love, that I was blessed and that paradise was open to me as long as I agreed to recognize that the truest part of me was something else, different from the character I was portraying down here in this human tragedy. I felt like blaspheming and saying the real me wasn't part of this world ... and that it would continue to exist once the curtain had fallen on my life.

CHAPTER 27

The Buckwheat Blessing

THE ORIGINAL IDEA FOR THE BUCKWHEAT BLESSING BREAKFAST came from the Americans. One day, long before CHEZ CORA was even the sprout of an idea, I saw the same kind of dish in a 24-hour breakfast restaurant. The dish was called "Pigs in the Blankets" and was made up of three big sausages rolled up in pancakes. This already heavy meal was accompanied by three syrups – strawberry, blueberry, and Vermont maple.

The moment Jack the Alligator licked his chops when he saw our buckwheat crêpes, the idea came back to me. Julia and I talked about it and decided the little piggies deserved better: a more refined *crêpe*, maybe made with wheat flour, or possibly delicious sausages in a buckwheat pancake. My spatula immediately began to flutter on the grill, trying to imprison the piggies in the *crêpes*. Since every time one or the other would manage to free its foot or its tail or its ear, Julia decided to add some shredded cheddar which, as it melted, would serve as a kind of glue and hold our pudgy victims in their crisp shrouds.

Once they were on the plate, we accompanied our sausages with a nice mountain of cut fruit. Julie suggested we sprinkle some more shredded cheddar on the rolled sausage and *voilà!* The treat was born. There was no way we could call a Quebecois *crêpe* THE ALLIGATOR so we named the dish BUCKWHEAT BLESSING. Even today, this unusual combination of ingredients doesn't disappoint. With real maple syrup or, as some prefer, topped with traditional molasses, this dish is an ingenious example of CORA's magic.

CHAPTER 28

Discovering Custard

AFTER WE'D BEEN RUNNING *CHEZ CORA* FOR EIGHTEEN months, survival was starting to become less worrisome. We were now certain that we could pay all our bills and invested, within reason, in a few little extras: nice fabric for new aprons, a few cookbooks, and, most important of all, new exotic fruit that would wow our customers and keep them from going elsewhere.

I enjoyed staying in the snack bar after closing. For long hours, I would search for inspiration: in my own head, in books, in memories of walking through food markets, and in the stories about food my customers would share with me. I searched everywhere a new idea could be found and examined recipes for ways of combining two elements in order to create a third. And I always found something, a firecracker or a spark that would let the rabbit out of the hat the next day.

I got into the habit of drawing our new dishes on a

big white poster board. It didn't cost much. They served as a menu, and, as the customers said, it was an original idea. I really enjoyed the long evenings I spent thinking and drawing, swimming in the smell of paint. Sometimes I would think of Sister René-Goupil, my literature teacher in school, who always said, "Cora, your ideas are wonderful, but, my God, is your handwriting ever atrocious!"

It probably would have been good for me to relearn to draw each letter, to play with the *A*'s swollen torso, the stubborn *E*s, and the rigid bellies of the capital *B*s which had to balance without tumbling one onto the other. I always touched everything up, adding a pear or a cherry, a bird that had just flown in from Fort Lauderdale, or a four-tined fork next to the Mirella crêpes we had just invented for the tall, pretty girl who worked at Steilman Mode.

Mirella crêpes were made with whole wheat flour, which we'd created to help encourage Mirella in her weekly aerobics class, and, in our own way, to contribute to the well-being of our customers.

Mirella had told her friend Gordon about *Chez Cora*, and he showed up superbly dressed, with a brooch on his coat. It was the first time we'd seen a boy dressed like that, and we would never forget it. Gordon left us another unforgettable thing: custard. Yes indeed! He was the one who brought its sweetness into our lives, telling us about the gigantic feasts the *Auberge des Trois Saumons* served its rich summer clientele.

Gordon closed his eyes as he described to us the smooth white cream as it lazily dripped across the beautiful golden slices of a steaming French toast chateau that an artistic chef placed on a huge tray flooded with strawberry syrup. We all noticed the ecstasy on his face as he remembered the treat. Julia was the first one to declare that we, too, were capable of making such an elixir.

I had to search much farther afield than the *blanc-mange* I was served by the nuns during my teenage years. I climbed mountains of sugar calories, conquered long cooking times in a double boiler, and considered the multiple characteristics of egg yolks as they boil as I stubbornly chased after the savoury creaminess handsome Gordon had described. This thrilling journey allowed us to discover a precious ally in "Miss Pure Vanilla," along with a foolproof way of thickening milk that I will tell my grandchildren on my deathbed.

A few days later, Gordon returned to *Chez Cora* like a child who'd been promised the moon. And there he found it, dripping down the beautiful mound of fruit atop his Sunday French toast.

Julia waited for ecstasy to reappear on the visitor's thin face. And that is exactly what happened, almost immediately, when his fork placed the first piece of custard-covered bread in his mouth. This time, his happiness was noisy and punctuated by big shouts of *Bravo!*, between mouthfuls wrapped up in sauce, in a voice that sounded like a satisfied Santa Claus.

Of course we baptised the new custard with the name of the one who'd instigated its invention, and for a number of years, we used that name in honour of our precious customer, Gordon.

It wasn't the old queen of England who would later make us change the name of the sauce, but Nicholas, my youngest son and the young king of our operation. He felt service in the restaurant would be more efficient if the staff didn't have to explain that Gordon cream was a kind of custard, only better because the founder of the company and her daughter had invented it. So the damned need for efficiency resulted in the renaming of that beautiful sauce.

CHAPTER 29

Four Big Christmas Trees

WE STARTED TO BECOME MORE AND MORE DARING. AS I WAS cutting Christmas tree-shaped cookies from the molasses batter in December 1989, I got the idea of setting up four six-foot-tall Christmas trees in the little restaurant. Declaring my intention stirred up a lot of excitement in the snack bar.

"Boss, you must have fallen on your head again when you were putting up your menu signs!" exclaimed Platon, our new Caribbean dishwasher.

Down on all fours on the living room floor of our apartment, leaning over a big piece of bright green fabric, I cut out the huge trees we eventually put up, when the time was right, in the side windows of the restaurant. In the weeks leading up to Christmas, every night I decorated the trees with multicoloured rounds of felt, garlands of mismatched ribbons, snowflakes made from white batting, little stars made out of yellow satin, silvery buttons, real little candy canes, and eight little cotton birds with pink feathers that old Mrs. Edmond had brought me one day — "in case they could be of any use in the restaurant."

The trees were planted just a few days before Christmas, one in each window frame, just within reach of the hands of the children who were allowed to touch the creations as long as they waited until the day after Christmas to remove the red and white candy canes. At the top of each tree, a big yellow brocade star sat comfortably, as if resting after climbing up all by itself.

Among all the customers who had enjoyed the molasses cookies, not one dared to believe the cook's promise. They expressed surprise when they actually saw the trees. Each face offered a broad smile, a laugh, a bravo, or a "Thank you, Cora!" The multicoloured forest ironically turned out to be a wonderful gift for me because, from that day on, it lived in my head. And every time I called it up before my eyes, I would be amazed by the extraordinary power of a creative imagination.

***

Despite the dollars that were making their way into our cash register, we weren't really working at Côte-Vertu or running a business or, thanks be to God, getting rich. The restaurant had become our own kitchen, private library, and living room — we were living there. We welcomed people as if they were members of our familes and we were sincerely interested in each one of their stories. Some days, it seemed like serving food was nothing but a pretext for having people over and that our breakfasts were magic tricks we used to amaze our guests. Offering ten kinds of fruit in a crêpe or on French toast was our own way of being generous; just like "two eggs with bacon" was our way of saying "*Bonjour.*"

CHAPTER 30

Visiting the Lettuce

SOMETIMES, I'D COME UP WITH A NEW DISH JUST SO THE vision would stop bouncing around in the tight space behind my eyes. I liked to draw words and invent lives for them, but I especially liked to discover new creatures and describe them with old-fashioned adjectives and verbs that oozed magic. I enjoyed spending time illustrating a piece of fruit, imagining its great-uncles, distant cousins, brothers, and even the bastard offspring that science dared offer to consumers.

Once, I spent several days with the lettuce family, looking for a courageous little servant that could hold up the orange wedge we served with our egg dishes. This is how I ended up testing several different types of lettuce, indeed over twenty different kinds of the leafy plants, some tender, others crunchy. I touched at least a dozen of them before I came across some good old chicory, while I was visiting displays of iceberg lettuce.

Strong, thin, lacy, pointed leaves formed a voluminous plant whose cheerful appearance was in sharp contrast to the yellow dullness of the tight-hearted iceberg. The chicory leaf, which remains shiny and splendidly green all year long, became the perfect accompaniment for the orangey smile of our morning fruit citrus for many years.

I was always looking for new knowledge, for a new surprise, or a particular way of cutting fruit and vegetables that would keep the seeds from splitting or keep the tomato from bleeding. I heard about a monstrous kind of technology that promised to extend the shelf life of vegetables by reducing the amount of oxygen they breathe. And I would feel sorry for my silly leeks because their bodies were always stuffed with sand, despite the many turbans they had on their heads.

"What good does it do to be wearing so many clothes, if you're always up to your navel in mud?" Julia asked me, upset.

"It makes you handsome and delicious in the vichyssoise," replied Mary E. Falcon, a steady customer, her ear anxious to dive into a conversation.

Mary E. had probably never put a cream of potato through a sieve, but she knew every aspect of home making by heart. She had been a boarder for fifteen years before she took up conjugal duties under the direction of a certain Lady B. Falcon and her son, who had had the good fortune of securing a position as an

Army officer at twenty-three, along with the ill fortune of dying at twenty-eight, leaving his low ranking wife under the yoke of her exceptionally rich Irish mother-in-law.

Late in the afternoon, I would stroll down supermarket aisles. I would read all the labels on the different brands of jellies and jams. I'd discretely sniff the powdered chicken bouillon in its transparent containers. Sometimes on Thursday or Friday night, I'd trade a few hours of sleep for two or three Cantonese chicken drumsticks at the Sainte Catherine market. I'd keep my eye on the new items and the prices of different foods – the price of pineapple for example, which I'd only buy when it was heavy, free of bruises, and sporting the beautiful, dark green leaves I'd use to garnish our fresh fruit dishes, and that I would later plant in our MAGIC breakfasts. I crisscrossed the city. In the Armenian neighbourhood around Salaberry Boulevard, at Mourelatos supermarket, in the Italian neighbourhood near Jean-Talon market, I'd look for foods that were more likely to arouse the appetite than satisfy hunger. I'd often go to Milano, on Saint-Laurent Street, a real treasure trove for an apprentice cook, where all my senses would be delighted: the warm welcome, the personalized service, the huge choice of cold cuts, cheeses, oils, and pastas, and what a choice of typically Italian vegetables! I was constantly open to new ideas.

Now there were a few dollars relaxing in the account at the bank. I could buy red pepper to add a bang to our western omelettes; choose seedless grapes for the clothes maker Michel's young children to enjoy safely; buy myself a few bottles of Windex – with the squirt trigger included – to lighten my dear Marie's work load.

I still didn't have time to write stories, but I did read every food magazine published in Canada. I also started to buy my first American magazines, publications with superb illustrations where renowned chefs were beginning to talk about the best breakfasts in the world.

In those new moments of happiness, I'd catch myself thinking that maybe the planet was not as hostile as I had thought, after all. Sometimes, I'd completely forget my fight against the evil spirits, and I'd stubbornly try to discover what would make me happy. And I still managed to get the *béchamel* sauce to stick, to knock over the sugar tart in the oven, or, worst of all, to break the famous fan vent.

"We can never be happy for too long before something awful happens to us," my mother used to warn us.

She also said it was a bad idea to laugh too much one day, because you might end up with something to cry about the next.

"When things are going too well," Mélie Barthelot from Caplan used to repeat, "the devil steps right in and gives you a black eye."

Above all, we couldn't let ourselves believe we were

the good ones, God's chosen, because we were far from fulfilling all the necessary conditions to enter the kingdom of heaven.

"God's logic is incomprehensible to humans," good Father Antoine used to say during my classical studies.

I supposed that's why he later gave up his robe and married the nun who disembowelled the frogs in chemistry class. Still, Father Antoine was a superior being, according to the nuns; a holy man into whose ear we spilled our sinful souls' worst calamities; a man of God who urged us to repent and forced us to say two rosaries, on our knees, with our eyes fixed on the lighted picture of hell painted on the ceiling of the school's little chapel. Those frightening, macabre images of hell were recorded in the hearts of all of us schoolgirls, unable as we already were to please the real God.

The Greek wedding, in 1967. Cora officially became Mrs. Tsouflidou.

In 1987, Cora and Marie, behind the counter of the first Chez Cora on Côte-Vertu, in Saint Laurent.

Titan, Cora's eldest son, with Cora's first grandchild born in 1989.

Julia, Cora's daughter, handling the training of a group of future employees. A franchising necessity!

Nicholas (centre) training other cooks in the network in 1992.

Nicholas is promoted to Director of Operations of the network in 2000.

Chez Cora advertising campaign billboards.

CHAPTER 31

The Surprise Breakfast

Sometimes, I would step away from my griddle for a few hours, and give the little waitress an opportunity to practice flipping omelettes without breaking them. This gave me the chance to go out in the wide world to see if there was anything besides the daily grind. At that time, this desire to flee resulted in me wandering from one end of the Sainte Catherine market to the other, which was a bubbling den of flavours. I'd travel from one continent to the next, tossed about in an elevator, or rising bodily on an escalator. It was in this strange state of experiencing foreign travel in my own city that I first saw a tiny Miraclean griddle wedged in between a long row of Egyptian delicacies and a thick window facing the street. Above it a huge sign that said Eggs had just been hung.

On the hot surface which still hadn't been marred by even the tiniest scratch, a young Lebanese man with a strange wooden spatula was trying to flip – without breaking – a sandwich whose stuffing immediately caught my attention.

"Young man, please tell me what's in the sandwich."

"It's a breakfast sandwich, madame. Breakfast is our specialty."

"Very interesting, young man. And tell me, how long have you been the breakfast expert in this city?"

"Since we opened this counter, two weeks ago!"

There was something to be admired about the young man's courage. So I ordered a "morning sandwich" and since I was then the only customer at the counter, it was easy for me to observe Maroum Ouahim as he prepared his specialty. Two thick slices of bread were placed buttered-side-down on the grill. On each one, he placed a thin slice of yellow cheese. Then he placed a pre-prepared over easy egg on one slice and a slice of ham on the other. He closed the sandwich with his spatula and then pressed down on it, horror of horrors! (Pressing down on a hamburger is what you do to flatten it out as it cooks.)

The sandwich finally made its way into my mouth, crunchy with flavour, but much too well-done to satisfy a gourmand's palate.

"Thank you very much, Maroum! By the way, if you ever want to find a job closer to home, I have a little snack bar on the corner of Côte-Vertu and Montpellier in Saint-Laurent."

Before it made its way onto our griddle, Maroum's morning sandwich was dunked in French toast batter so its walls would be sealed and the cheese wouldn't run out. When it was cooked, the mixture of eggs and sugar gave the sandwich a very surprising flavour. We decided to call it the SURPRISE breakfast, as a surprise for the young Lebanese man if he ever happened to wander into our place.

CHAPTER 32

A Faithful Ambassador

EVERYONE IN THE SNACK BAR THOUGHT MARY E. FALCON WAS our most devoted ambassador because whenever she'd hear that the Saint-Laurent fire hall was ordering lunch on the phone, she'd always volunteer to go deliver it. The 58-year-old woman really did help when she stepped into the station with huge portions of steaming spinach lasagne. And it certainly also helped the delivery woman's morale when she relived, only for an instant, the admiration of men in uniform. Mary E. secretly loved Marcel, a handsome firefighter, and was the only one who didn't notice how strange it was that they were always both at the snack bar at the same time. The attractive man had already been married twice in the last four years and would brag about how familiar he was with all the ins and outs of a woman's soul.

"And of fire hydrants," I'd add in my head, on those

rare occasions when I could follow the conversation from my kitchen.

Even though he was always the first one to tell dirty jokes, Marcel was also the Jaws of Life specialist in Saint-Laurent. His coworkers told the story of how, the year before, Marcel had to extricate an Asian woman cut in two from the wreckage of a brand new Honda Prelude on the Metropolitaine highway as her greenish intestines dangled over the railing, right at the Décarie interchange.

"That kind of situation is worse than fire!" the brave Marcel concluded, after acting out the incident for the hundredth time.

Mary E. would bring us back the money from the delivery, and she'd also give us the tip money that a woman of her ill-defined status couldn't accept. Sometimes, at the end of the day, she'd suggest we go have something to eat at *Wings and Things* or at *Cicerone*, the Italian restaurant on Henri-Bourassa Boulevard. She wanted to get to know me, she'd say, to understand how I managed to be satisfied with the snack bar. She wanted to know if there was a man in my life, and what kind of awful husband could have abandoned a woman as brave as me.

I was also was fascinated by her existence and how she'd managed to remain in her mother-in-law's service for so long while getting older with no husband or child. I supposed we each had what the other didn't. Damn planet – it was again having fun by making us think we were incomplete, because we didn't have what we would probably never need. Damn dinners with Mary E. Betty, Martin, and later on with Martha! Damn devil – once again, under pretence of pleasant conversation, insidiously infecting our brains, spreading doubt, fear, and those awful seeds of despair! The handsome customer Marcel was probably right – it was better to make love than pretend to be intellectual and have deep discussions with one's fellow creatures.

"The trouble with you women," Marcel would confirm, "is that you get carried away too easily with each other's problems, and what you call compassion is a kind of frustration that eventually flips over and knocks you in the head!"

Sometimes, I wondered what would happen if we really managed to believe that love was the only important thing, that we'd never been kicked out of paradise, that we are happy and that all that stuff about the Last Judgment is nothing but a huge trick designed by one group to have better control over another. Maybe I'd never find what I was missing because I really wasn't missing anything. If love was the only important thing, there would be no gates in front of heaven, God would be everywhere, and there would be no hell. If love was the only important thing, I'd be an angel and my heart would always be filled with God, peace, and contentment. But all that is impossible, My imperfections, my bad thoughts, my failures and my ignorance proved to me every day that I still had a long way to go. I was undoubtedly unworthy, but ultimately what I wanted most in the world was to get as close as possible to God and His heaven.

CHAPTER 33

Dream-filled Moments

ONE DAY, MARY E. FALCON ANNOUNCED TO EVERYONE THAT a regular customer known to us all as Syndicat (nicknamed thus because of his involvement with labour unions) wanted to marry me and that I'd probably become the third living wife of an Arab taxi driver. Oh yes! I loved his dark eyes traced in a face the colour of eggplant roasted on a griddle. I especially loved the velvety way he talked on the quieter mornings when the city traffic left him time to sip a few teas flavoured with fresh mint. I would buy the tea especially for him, and Mary predicted that the little bouquet of aromatic leaves would soon be traded for a bridal bouquet. Syndicat and I would play around and pretend she was right, teasing and laughing about how I didn't care about his other obligations and that he could always find a few extra trips between Dorval and Sainte-Marie Place so that he and I could eventually enjoy the warm sands of al-Manãma.

These dream-filled moments broke up the occasional boredom of the snack bar like magnificent transatlantic cruise ships, pulling along in their wake fictional romances, fantasies, and dreams that would never come true. I liked Syndicat, it's true, but I also liked Yvon from Taxi Champlain and Frank from Canadair. I liked them all and I tried to understand why Mary E. so vehemently refused to offer a smile, a caressing look, or even half her butter pat to a stranger sitting next to her. Personally, I refused to believe you had to be married to offer the opposite sex some of the sweetness that is so necessary in life. I gave advice about feeding newborns to Frank without even touching the tip of his finger, because his wife worked nights at the Sainte-Justine Hospital and he would spend his afternoons fighting with the different things the nurse had scribbled on all his baby's bottles. Without having Mary E. find out, I even cooked Yvon's Christmas turkey in the snack bar oven, because his sweetheart also worked at night, but at a different kind of hospital, called the Cabaret Paré (a nightclub with nude dancers in the centre of Montreal). I wrapped hundreds of portions of homemade *cretons* in clear, little plastic containers so the guys would have some at home on the weekends and they could give a taste to their girlfriends, their wives, or any friends who still didn't know our address. I did everything I could to make them happy and, when I'd get to the bottom of my bag of tricks, I'd start all over again and try new ways to make love blossom. And, I must confess, I also liked all the stories Mary E. made up about my various adventures.

Late in 1989, I had the feeling that a new planet was starting to sprout beneath the Côte-Vertu parking lot and that its favourable wind would soon cross my threshold.

CHAPTER 34

The Samira Wake-Up

One morning a man of about fifty, with a dark, hot face, showed up in the restaurant doorway. His face was split in the middle by a huge moustache above an irresistible smile. The man hesitated a few seconds before entering, finally giving in to the aroma of nutmeg coming from a dish of oatmeal that had just been served at the counter. From his appearance, it seemed that he was a refugee from a noble family, used to more luxurious establishments. He walked towards the counter and had to step over old Sarto's cane to take a seat. For a few seconds, he stared at the crêpes being flipped on the big griddle and then asked, "Some fruit... nice and fresh, if possible, please."

"Fresh!" replied Marie, as if she'd found a tarantula in the sugar bowl. "My goodness, we have nothing *but* fresh fruit. How could you not know that? Where have you been?"

And that's how Mr. Samira came to tell us he was an immigrant florist who was enjoying a certain success on Décarie Boulevard at Saint-Laurent. Samira's request led us to serve him a beautiful plate of nothing but pretty, cut fruit, no crêpes, no cheese, no French toast. Because that was his favourite dish in Beirut, back when his mother would bring him the same glass dish full of peaches, apricots, and purple-fleshed figs.

We named the dish we served that day SAMIRA WAKE-UP because of the Lebanese florist, and for a long time our drawing of it had a row of multicoloured tulips under the words.

CHAPTER 35

The Ten Story Omelette

A FEW DAYS LATER, THE CONSTRUCTION BOSS FROM THE TENTH story of the building going up across the street landed on our doorstep. Marie jumped when she noticed the fellow straddling the first stool at her counter. Lightweight, with a powdery complexion, the man had a strange way of moving his hair as he tried to decipher the menu. He was looking for an omelette. When he finally spoke to the waitress, his voice was so soft, Marie swallowed a few flies before she got control of herself again.

"We only have three kinds of omelettes, sir. And, don't look for newspapers, I forgot to get them this morning."

"With cheese and fried potatoes," the customer finally said with a slightly ungrateful face. "And a hot chocolate because I don't want to be shaky when I walk across the beam on the tenth floor."

The unpredictable Marie immediately fell for this construction cowboy. She told him about the mischief the electricians got up to and, without my knowing it, she also shared the spicy stories the firefighters had told her that very morning. Antoine and his crew of masons quickly became regular morning customers. They'd sit at the round table in the front of the restaurant, muttering quietly as they sipped their warm drinks. Their calm, docile manner made it easy to see why they were masters of the heights. I watched them from the back of my kitchen. They sat hunched over, almost quiet, looking like a flock of huge birds wisely sitting on a parapet.

One Saturday afternoon, Antoine came to the snack bar alone and spoke to me for the first time. He was working overtime. The building construction was coming to a close and the foreman from Laduco had noticed some unusual spending for asbestos sheets used to make the elevator shaft. Antoine had spent the afternoon detailing the past of each of his men and assuring him of the integrity of the team he'd been working with for more than eight years.

"I told him, 'You should check out the tinsmiths, and just let my guys get back to calmly stacking their bricks,'" declared Antoine as if he were talking to a judge in a black robe. "What about you, Cora, do you accuse your waitress when you're short of flour for the crêpe batter? It's no use exaggerating. Saint-Marthe Stonework has to keep up its reputation! Twenty-five years of filling in the frameworks of buildings with bricks! And taller ones than the one across the street!"

Before my eyes, the man revealed a sudden vigour, spurred on by aggression and his recent insult. He described the questioning foreman like he was a step-father who'd caused him pain. Luckily, the snack bar was empty; as empty as the cowboy's stomach. He ordered his omelette. As I got busy, with slightly exaggerated sweetness, Antoine told me a bit about his life; how much he liked his coworkers and his Châteauguay suburban life. And he asked me to guess his favourite pastime.

"Yes, ma'am, I'm just like you: I love cooking!"

And without paying any attention to the beautiful Mirella who'd just come into the snack bar, the working man started to rattle off the recipe of his most successful masterpiece.

"I get everything from the fridge — ham, bacon, sausages that I cut into little slices, and even baloney when my wife agrees to buy some, and onions, tomatoes, pepper, cream, and cheese to grate over the omelette, which I serve in the biggest plate in the hutch. Let me tell you, I break four or five large eggs into a salad bowl, and I beat them together. I add the meat which I've cut into thin strips and sautéed in a pan with big pieces of vegetable. I add cream and some pepper, because I don't eat anything without pepper, and I pour the whole thing into Josianne's late grandmother's cast iron pan; and I wait for as long as it takes to fill the percolator and make seven or eight pieces of toast. Then, I call my wife to get her out of bed, she can't resist my omelettes. And then, Cora, with all due respect, we eat the best omelette in the world! Oh, I almost forgot, sometimes I even add fresh spinach leaves to the mix, when Carméla hasn't eaten them all as part of her Hollywood diet! Still, she's never going to make any movies, and there's no doubt she cheats on Saturdays. I put the plate on the mauve table in the kitchen. My father says that mauve colour is an unusual one for people like us from Shawinigan. Really, you ought to make my omelette here, in your restaurant. The guys would fall on the floor, or else they wouldn't be able to move a single brick! It's up to you! I'm just a mason in charge of the tenth floor at Laduco. I eat here because it makes me think of home... and because you make me think of my mother. You make the same crêpes she used to make. I can't be the first person to say that to you."

As Antoine listed the ingredients for his omelette, I was putting them into the mixing bowl. Then, I placed his favourite omelette on the counter in front of him. After we both thanked each other, we decided to come up with a name for the new breakfast.

"Either the ANTOINE OMELETTE or the TEN STORY," I suggested.

"Call it the TEN STORY... for all the guys from Sainte-Marthe Stoneworks who've bashed their bones regrouting all the walls of the tenth story at Laduco."

"I promise I will, Antoine! I'll call it the TEN STORY OMELETTE. And anyone who doesn't know the story will think it's because of all the ingredients."

Thanks to Antoine, a new successful breakfast was added to our repertoire.

CHAPTER 36

EGGS MAURICE

ONE DAY, SOMEONE ATTENDING A LECTURE BY NAPOLEON HILL asked him to share his recipe for the easiest way to make money. The famous motivational speaker didn't even pause to think before he said, "My friends, right now, go to any city you want, settle in and then take a few days to observe what the population needs the most. Get it yourself and offer it to the people. That's the best way to get rich!"

One morning, what Germaine Pock needed to convince her husband to accompany her on her Sunday pilgrimage to *Chez Cora* was my promise that we'd add big, well-cooked, smoked sausages to the choice of meats we served in the morning. Her square-headed giant of a husband had been brought up with big wieners and had eaten thousands of them in his lifetime. At over fifty years old, and despite his wife Germaine's skilled fingers in the kitchen, Maurice insisted on cooking his own sausages at least once a week on Sundays, with the four scrambled eggs he consumed as his usual ration of cholesterol.

"Yes! Germaine, I promise we'll have smoked sausages on next Sunday's menu!"

"They can't be that hard to find!" added Evelyne, with the seriousness of a school teacher. "We'll call our Maurice from Delipro. I'm sure he knows about sausages, too!"

A week later, when Germaine's Maurice showed up on our doorstep, he looked more like a Key West lifeguard than an old sausage eater from Cornwall. His shape was like a Greek god, and perfectly smoked, too, and he had two little hazelnuts looking out from under his eyelids. Sniffing at the new environment, Maurice soon settled himself on the vacant stool closest to the kitchen.

By serving him his heart's desire, we not only earned ourselves a new customer, but we also invented a new breakfast plate which, of course, we baptised EGGS MAURICE.

The more sausages we sold, the fresher they were; the fresher they were, the more we sold; the more we sold the more money we made. Napoleon Hill had sure been right.

CHAPTER 37

CITRUS BALLERINA

USING THE MOST UNEXPECTED CIRCUMSTANCES OR THE funniest creatures as inspiration, I aimed to make each customer's plate the shape of a wish. I learned this from what a plumber told me about grapefruit, which he never managed to finish before.

I peeled the big citrus fruit and cut it into slices that I would alternate with orange slices in a pretty see-through plate. Then I put a chicory leaf near the acidic segments, along with a big juicy strawberry with its belly spread out like a fan. The plumber, nicknamed Ballerina because of a Halloween photo of him in a pink ballet costume he'd once shown us, was immediately delighted by the looks of the dish, and by the opportunity to eat up his potassium in such pleasant company. Ballerina remained a faithful client of the snack bar for a long time; from time to time, he would clear a pipe or fix the freezer siphon for absolutely nothing because we'd helped him eat his vitamins. He later came back to look after the plumbing changes at the second CHEZ CORA, insisting on being paid at a discount.

"Out of solidarity," he specified, "because you deserve to succeed, and because, among my customers, there are those who have the means to more than make up for it."

CHAPTER 38

A Clan of Gazelles

ADÉLAÏDE PARFUM ALSO HAD A BALLERINA IN HER FAMILY of five beautiful daughters. With her imposing stature and heavy, gravelly voice, Mrs. Parfum majestically managed her clan of gazelles. She herself decided what each one wanted and also coordinated the expenses and movements of her offspring. That's how she ended up at our place, one Sunday morning in September, while she was waiting for the sale at the *Dans un jardin* perfume factory to start. She'd decided that perfume for six women had to be purchased at a discount and, to soften her decision, she'd agreed to invite her five young ladies to the famous snack bar her husband was always defending so faithfully. She wanted to see for herself if the quality of our fruit was as good as her Jean-Claude said, and to sample the crêpe dishes that would make her ancestors roll over in their graves.

Mrs. Parfum arrived first with the family's young

children, the twins Janette and Ginette. The three eldest, Jovette, Josée, and Jacynthe, lived in an apartment in the basement of her brother-in-law's duplex in Saint-Laurent.

"They should be here," declared the mother, projecting her voice into the kitchen to get my attention. "The little villains want to get perfume without getting out from under the blankets! Ginette! Janette! Split a dish of blueberry crêpes," ordered the corporal, now on a roll. "We'll see if there's any real butter around here!"

My Julia loved that kind of trouble-maker! And she decided to confront her. She had even sacrificed the snack bar's only two tables for four to welcome the Parfum dynasty. And she had no intention of needlessly wasting her precious seats.

"Ma'am?" Julia asked.

"I'm waiting for my daughters," replied Adélaïde.

"I'm sorry, but you have to order right away, we can't hold the table any longer!" Julia ordered.

"Excuse me? What did you say?" asked Mrs. Parfum.

And, just as Julia was about to let loose with her own bucket of spicy comments, a sudden aroma of spring flowers entered *Chez Cora*.

"Jovette!" exclaimed Julia, looking at the front door. "I never expected to see you here. Hmm! This is your mother? Pleased to meet you! I... hmm! I've known Jovette for a long time... Yes, yes, at school," Julia went on.

"This is Josée, my sister, the dancer," said Jovette, making the introductions.

"Pleased to meet you, I admire ballerinas," added my daughter, to be polite. "Mom! This is Josée Parfum, my friend Jovette's sister!"

"I didn't know we had common ground," said General Parfum. "My husband comes here sometimes with the guys from Canadair. It's nice! And he says it's good!"

"Dad had your blueberry crêpes and he says they're even better than at the hotel," exclaimed the young Ginette enthusiastically.

"We'll all try them, this morning, to see if he's right," ordered Adélaïde Parfum. "Four plates, 'cause the little ones will split one."

"Right!" said Julia. "Would you like orange juice with that?"

"No, no, we had some at home," the heavy woman replied with a question on her face. "And there's sauce for the crêpes, too, right? Cordon sauce?"

"Gordon," Julia corrected. "It's like a custard, absolutely delicious with all our crêpe or French toast dishes!"

"We want it!" begged the five Parfum mouths with one voice.

"My mother likes me to say it's flavoured with vanilla," added Julia to satisfy Mrs. Parfum's nose.

The members of the aromatic dynasty stuffed their faces and everyone in the snack bar was very satisfied.

The younger Parfum ladies became faithful ambassadors for our blueberry crêpes covered in custard. Josée, the ballerina, came back often with other celebrities from the artistic community. And it was at our counter that she met Redgy, her future husband, when she simply asked him to pass her the ketchup.

The invisible orchestra leader had a huge success when he decided to start a symphony in the snack bar. He would bring back together people who had been friends for a long time or introduce future husbands and wives, whether they were ready for it or not.

CHAPTER 39

Merle Manzi

ON DAY THE INVISIBLE ANGEL BROUGHT IN MERLE MANZI – a private detective I had met on a visit to Boston – into the snack bar. Merle was glued to a counter in Quincy market where he was eating ribs with hot sauce, when my sandal strap caught on the spur of his crocodile skin boot. I just barely had time to wonder why a group of big men was gathered around a spinning machine (used to grill the biggest ribs in the American northeast) when the stranger to whose shoe I was now attached said, "Yes, ma'am! It's good!"

"Sir! My shoe is stuck to your boot."

"Lady, I'm eating!" proclaimed a mouth hole disconnected from the rest of the body.

"Please, sir, listen to me! My shoe is stuck to yours."

"Lady, you must have one of these delicious ribs."

When I returned from my long weekend in the

United States, I'd done such a good job describing Merle to my daughter Julia that, when he showed up in our little restaurant without warning, she immediately recognized him.

Without missing a beat, she called to him, "Merle Manzi! Hi! How are you, sir?"

The American detective froze in his tracks and almost dropped dead right there in front of Julia. Since I'd seen him, he'd been promoted to the CIA and was in Montreal on a "top secret" mission. I had given him the address of the snack bar and he thought he'd take advantage of his hour off to come and dust off his spurs with me. And here he was being recognized by a stranger; a young girl, whose exotic looks could easily make her a member of the group of Mexican students he was searching for, who were then threatening the life of his president. And now he was being recognized!

"Sir, please have a seat, we know you here. We were expecting you'd come in one of these days. Have some coffee, Mr. Manzi! Please sit down! Let me take your briefcase, and sit. We also have hot chocolate. You are Merle Manzi, aren't you? Please answer, Mr. Manzi."

But the detective remained dumbfounded. Not knowing which way was up, he leaned on the edge of the counter and asked to use the phone. Julia suggested that he should come with her into the kitchen, where the only phone was located. The man refused to move and that's how I found him, stunned, when I came up from the basement, my hands full of multicoloured fish, since that was the French tradition on April Fool's Day, which was the next day.

"Merle Manzi! Long time no see!"

"Co... Co... Cora?! Wow, it is you! Darling, how are you?"

Fear quickly drained from the American police officer. Merle gobbled up several crêpes, and asked me out for dinner. According to the local police officers at Station 53, the best steakhouse in town was on Saint-Laurent Boulevard.

The police officers were right, because I'd never been treated as well as in Moishe's Steakhouse where two or three servers always keep an eye on your table: one for the water, one for the pickles, and one for the order. When the steaks came, the big, long-toothed knives followed close behind. Merle perspired as he contemplated the thickness of the meat.

He abruptly grabbed the sharp weapon and began to puff as he tore into his steak like a lion eating a gazelle.

Merle refrained from ordering any wine since he'd gotten into the habit of not drinking wine on duty. With my eyes on the grooves in his neck, I continued to watch, as a barely chewed Napoleon pastry slipped down his throat. Without knowing exactly why, I suddenly decided that in two minutes, I was going to stand up, claim sudden illness and get away from the famous restaurant and its crimson velvet wainscoting.

Back at the snack bar despite the late hour I hung eighteen big paper fish, ready for the next day's festivities, over the tables and the counter; nice, pretty fish floating through their night, as free as I was.

Merle disappeared into the crowd like all the other Romeos who'd come into the snack bar before him. As far as I was concerned, I had once again escaped the horns of a bull.

The morning of April Fool's Day, I served the businessmen at the counter water-filled soup bowls with a real fish swimming in them, enjoying my precious imagination at the same time. I was convinced that one day my short stories would be ripe enough to take flesh. All I had to do was wait for the angel to light the lamp over my page.

CHAPTER 40

April 89

The large, well-filled April 89 crêpe came to us the day after our regulars found real goldfish in their soup. It was a little practical joke on my part. Betty, our favourite divorcee, thought we owed her a big favour because of the piscine trauma of the day before.

"Yes, Betty, ask me for anything you want, and I'll make it."

"Hmmm!"

Betty's lips turned on themselves a couple of times before they settled into the shape of a little red-painted spout. Shyly, "Maybe this" and "Maybe that" slipped from the opening several times. Then suddenly, pushed forward by her tongue, the following phrase poured out, "I can't make up my mind, Cora. I want crêpes and I also want fruit, but in my opinion it's not fattening enough to make up for your live fish joke. Couldn't you add some cream to it?"

"Leave it to me, Betty. Close those pretty blue eyes and wait — I promise you're going to pop your cork!"

The pretty customer had just given me an idea. Instead of cooking three crêpes and serving them with the usual amount of fruit, I spread a thin crêpe across the griddle and let it cook on one side before turning it over. Then I covered the cooked side with confectioner's custard and poured on the portion of fruit; I folded each side of the crispy crêpe towards the middle as if to hide the filling, and I placed the delicious gift on a big oblong plate. Topped with a whipped cream rosette and a sprinkling of snow (powdered sugar), the new breakfast caused several explosions in my brain before Betty could even touch it with her fork. When the utensil lifted its first sample of food, dozens of hungry eyes were fixed on the young divorcée's open mouth.

"Mmmm!" exclaimed Betty. "I'll swallow a goldfish every day if you keep making me treats like this the next! It's divine!"

It was, and that memorable date was also the first time I used confectioner's custard in a crêpe. Betty herself suggested calling the new creation APRIL 89. Unanimously approved, the name was illustrated with pretty drawings of fruit and tacked up just next to the apple crêpe. It was fascinating to notice that each of the stars of our menu was the result of a moment when a client shared a dream about food. It showed how important it was to listen, and to pay as much attention to a face's trembling silence as to the words pouring from a hungry belly.

CHAPTER 41

My Head Above Water

In two years, *Chez Cora* had become my home and the place where everything important happened. It was my life in action and, thank God, in evolution. I didn't want to think of the unfortunate things that had happened in the past; not with Mary E. and not alone with myself. Now that I'd gotten my head above water, I only wanted to think about the future, about my children's tomorrows and their children's tomorrows. I started to think differently, to consider my little restaurant as a tool that I could use to build something bigger than our current comfortable situation.

I'd bought the place without seeing beyond the lines of the notebook I was writing in. But it seemed that the chapters were now starting to repeat themselves.

I cooked, I cleaned, I drew on the wall, and in my free time, I'd invent new breakfast or lunch dishes. I adored my customers and the fact that I was completely devoted to serving them. With my courage, as a mother hen and mother chef, I enthusiastically fed all the empty-bellied kids in the neighbourhood. And despite the deep satisfaction I was feeling, the warmth of the grill was starting to turn my eyes red a little too often. I noticed that the job's constant chattering was starting to slow down in my throat and grow more and more silent. From the counter, the carrot cake looked at me sadly from its plastic bubble: it was the first one to notice my eyes weren't as bright as they used to be, and that the narrowness of the space was starting to imprison me too. I'd sown two little silk carrots in place of the *T*s on the poster for the cake, but I was having trouble finding the same enthusiasm that had once inspired me. It was high time for a new miracle to occur.

***

The big plane swooped towards the ground. Titan was waiting for me at the end of the tunnel leading to the arrivals area. He lived in a little house, like a thousand others, on the highest hill in Atlanta. Behind it, in the middle of the family subdivision, was an immense blue swimming pool, and in the middle of the pool, after ten long months apart, I saw my Marie and her big belly floating, like a frog in the sun. My first grandchild, hidden in Marie's belly, was what made me think about enlarging my own space.

Titan showed me around the clean, prosperous, orderly city that lived and breathed business. He took me along the wide boulevards, into little cafés, showed me fudge stands and huge shopping malls. Since he was an advertising salesman, my son knew all the city's businesses by heart. Sure of himself, Titan would talk boldly about our American cousins. He shared with me his spectacular ideas for sandwich shops, black bean wraps, and subs he could make hundreds of combinations for. Titan dreamed of getting rich quick and making intercontinental trips. All I wanted to do was expand my lunch counter. I'd spent twenty-four months taming the residents of the henhouse and it seemed impossible to me to exchange all that for a bean-stuffed submarine adventure, or, worse still, to squeeze it into a Mexican sundried tomato pita.

When I got back from the United States, a new idea was taking root in my head. Julia promised me she could run the snack bar without me; she had even hired a young Moroccan immigrant named Moumou who made cakes as good as her mother's. I could go home, rest, and even write novels if I felt like it.

I didn't really think about writing, but my reading again shifted direction. Management theory replaced cookbooks, and rules of accounting replaced the alchemy of cooking. I was thinking. I was still working at the counter in the mornings, while Moumou cooked and Julia and Nicole, who had replaced Marie, waited on the tables. I'd leave early, at about one thirty, looking for the brilliant future that a lady client once found for me in the heart-shaped tea leaves at the bottom of my cup.

Our weekly sales meet our expenditures, but it was easy to see that the money would never stack up quickly enough to allow us to make many improvements to our situation. We also had to admit that the restaurant was too small, and we were constantly turning away new customers. People waiting in the lineups outside were always asking me to open another restaurant in their neighbourhood, near the Olympic stadium, on the south bank, in Laval or Lachine.

"Starting over again somewhere else! *Oof*!" I exclaimed.

"*Continuing* somewhere else," Julia corrected me.

"Because we're still going to call you every day to find out what soup to serve!" added Nicholas, wanting to encourage me.

I was looking for a new challenge. Since I'd survived the vagaries of burnout, sacrificing my writing, and the temptation of suicide on the stairs, I knew I probably had the where-with-all to keep going.

"We can increase what we're doing," Julia insisted. "The proof is that we've already started thinking about it," she added, convinced.

One day, a tarot card reader convinced me that business was part of my life path. According to the strange figures, in past lives I'd already tried my hand at the arts – theatre and writing to be exact. I had excelled at them and now it was time for me to master business.

"*Oof*! What karma," I answered.

All the sultans in my life disappeared when they saw my chef's coat replace the Madonna's veil. I had no one but my children to talk to about the new buds appearing on the branches of my thoughts. Still, one morning I opened up to our friendly coffee salesman, Mr. Van Foutte. We shared the secret of the half cases he'd sell me, against his company's policy. He was one of the first suppliers to knock on the door of the snack bar when it was undergoing renovation. He'd even offered to clean the antique coffee maker Machinpoulos had used to quench his clients' thirst.

Mr. Van Foutte knew all the little greasy spoons on Montreal island and beyond, including the ones on Ile-de-Jésus and on West Island, which, at that time, was his second territory. He was absolutely positive that we would succeed again, in a new location. And why not in a bigger place where we would be able to serve even more customers?

"And sell even more coffee!" added Julia to please the salesman.

I found a place on Saint-Laurent, near Crémazie; a restaurant that had only recently closed, but whose Italian owner was asking a high monthly rent because of all the equipment that was still there.

Mr. Van Foutte discouraged me from setting up a business there, citing the parking problems, and reminding me that the offices on Place-Crémazie had been half empty for quite some time.

"You have to be cautious about choosing the location for your second location," he added, promising to keep an eye open as he made his deliveries.

With my own eyes wide open, I searched the city, just receiving its first snow of the season. I walked down Fleury Street, Beaubien, Saint-Denis north of Jean-Talon West, the immigrant area of my past life. It seemed impossible to find a space that was as attractive as *Miss Côte-Vertu* had been. Still, I learned that the price per square meter of commercial property changed when the name of the street changed. And the closer I got to downtown, the more difficult it became to find something. It was discouraging, especially since the snack bar customers, urged on by my children, were now starting to discuss the next place where Mother Cora would crack her next egg.

As winter settled in, the intensity of my gaze lessened. Luckily, though, my destiny could still see far and wide. As far as Agadir, where Moumou's mother wanted her exiled son to return for his big sister's wedding. The cook's absence brought me back to the snack bar's pots and pans for three weeks.

"To warm up my feet," I delightedly thought.

And to notice that, even without its queen, the hive was still buzzing right along. Sales were on the rise and at noon new businessmen were arguing over the seats at the counter. A man called Léo had joined our crowd of regulars. He was crazy about our salmon pies, and according to Nicole, he usually gobbled one down with a double serving of egg béchamel.

Little by little, I rediscovered the excitement I'd known at the beginning. The last Thursday before Moumou's return, a young braggart sat down at our counter, just after the noon rush. He gulped down two Diet Cokes one after the other, then asked to speak to the boss. He had a snack bar to sell in Laval, in a little shopping center on Saint Martin Boulevard, across the street from some new office buildings. The man said he had a big counter with nine stools and enough tables for up to fifty people. I knew the place he was talking about. He kept his eyes fixed on me, as I was washing the yellow peas for the next day's soup.

"I'll give you everything in the restaurant for sixty thousand!"

I almost knocked over my pot of peas when he shot that price at me. No one had ever warmed the chairs of his richly coloured palace, except a few other people who were sick like I had been, and I knew this from first-hand experience. How could he dare ask so much?

"Sixty thousand dollars to have a famous Saint-Martin Boulevard address in Laval? It's a godsend, ma'am!"

Turned towards the inside of my head, my eyes started adding up our meagre savings. Between seven and eight thousand dollars was all we had in the world.

"A golden opportunity," the salesman insisted energetically.

He'd heard about our reputation and we were, according to his analysis, the best buyers for his business. Then the real tug-of-war began. I wanted to move forward, but I also wanted to stay where I was with all the people I loved so much. The kids were the ones who finally broke me out of my pensiveness; they wanted to go visit "our second *Chez Cora.*" They were excited by the location. And as for the price, hadn't I always told them that money was secondary? Out loud I thought, "Sixty thousand dollars for Saint-Martin Boulevard, for Laval, for Ile-de-Jésus, maybe it's worth going to take a look..."

Martine, a faithful customer, offered us her burgundy van so we could all go together that very afternoon. Sixty thousand dollars for a pool of ninety thousand people, as long as they liked us as much there as they did where we were? I started to consider it seriously.

By the time he left our counter, the salesman had us thinking that if we didn't buy his business, our future would be lost forever. But sixty thousand dollars! It was an astronomical sum for us.

"Julia, we'll go see it at four o'clock, I promise, cross my heart," I heard myself say.

As I crossed the Highway 15 bridge in Martine's burgundy van, I could see myself piling up egg cartons on the new Laval counter. I'd already mentally measured the front windows and put up flowered cotton valences. In front, near the cash register, there was even room for a little second-hand sofa recovered in the same fabric as the drapes. I'd have to hide the old fan, behind a wooden screen maybe, and put up wallpaper in the bathroom, to make it feel homey. We could also put jute along the lower half of the walls, and then put our pretty menu posters up like paintings. I could see the waitresses in black t-shirts, and big white aprons with CORA on embroidered them. I'd even put in my mother's hutch, which had been in our way since we'd sold the house in Boisbriand. We'd fill the window ledges with the big plastic chickens we'd just found at Goineau et Boursquet. There was so much room to draw, and it would mean no more trips through Montreal's freezing sludge.

When the vehicle came to a stop outside the new snack bar, my heart immediately stopped its purring. It was completely impossible to determine if heaven or hell had sent me such a troubling opportunity. Was it a sneaky ego waving this tantalizing but unattainable morsel before my eyes, or was it just destiny offering what it owed me? When I got out of the van, I felt like I was swimming in troubled waters. The bragging seller was ready to accept a small down payment. The rent was barely more than Côte-Vertu for twice the space and the owner of the shopping centre was going to let us open on Sundays despite the restriction on the current lease.

"We've given our suppliers so many free pieces of cake that they'll wait for us to pay for the equipment!"

Julia whispered to me soothingly.

Listening to the young seller, it again sounded like we'd have to say yes on the spot or go back home knowing full well we'd never do even a smidge better than the crappy little place we had. Still, I asked for time to think it over and promised to give my answer by Monday. I wanted to talk to Titan about it and he just happened to be on his way home. Since Marie insisted on giving birth in Quebec, they were expected to arrive late that night or early the next morning.

I had a hard time sleeping with that big YES I wanted to give dancing around in my stomach. I was waiting for the children and trying to put out the new fire that awful YES had lit in my head. I was thinking my mother would have said that it was impossible for it to happen that easily. That I shouldn't imagine that I would do any better than those who had come before me. That it was probably just another bout of boasting and that I'd regret getting caught up in the dance when the music stopped playing.

Still, I tried to find a response for each of my doubts, walking through the November cold, but probably not long enough. Would I have to get exhausted again, recite ten rosaries on my knees in front of an imposing picture of hell, and endure thirteen unending months of burnout before I could give birth to a new restaurant? My mother had died unexpectedly in a car accident. I'd had to identify her terrified face at the morgue, and the memory had stayed with me. Deep down, it was telling me that she certainly wasn't always right with her stories about having to pay your dues and her way of making us suffer in advance. Why did I always have to feel threatened by the morning after?

Nonetheless, it was the day after that put an end to my internal dilemma.

After travelling all night, Marie arrived at her mother's with her water broken. They had to move fast to get her to the hospital, and that's where Titan was when he called me at ten in the morning. I flew to Saint-Eustache and arrived just in time to see a nurse, on the other side of the nursery window, unwrapping what was going to be the biggest YES of the rest of my life.

Before my eyes, a little six-pound creature began to stretch his limbs as soon as the woman in white had freed him from his birthing blanket. Baby Alex had come into the world without causing his mother too much suffering and now it seemed like he was looking at me through the window! The grandmother that I became at that instant was encouraged by his little meows to move forward and say YES to the best reason in the world. As I was watching that little miracle, all wrapped in blue, I had the wonderful idea of transforming a grandma's big thanks into real support for underprivileged children. In my own way, I'd help feed as many children in need as possible. In fact, a few years later, I'd set up the CORA FOUNDATION whose only goal was giving breakfast to children who, for all sorts of reasons, come to school on an empty stomach.

CHAPTER 42

The Second Restaurant

I SAID YES AND THE PSYCHEDELIC CASTLE IN LAVAL WAS transformed into a warm, family diner. I sewed tablecloths and drapes, the waitresses' white aprons, and even a slipcover for an old second-hand loveseat. A friend gave us some wood slats so we could cover the ventilation hood and someone else gave us about twenty green bean boxes from Agripac and we used them as chicken cages. We put up harvest gold jute on the washroom walls and on the bottom half of the walls in the dining room. A number of customers from Saint-Laurent asked for the honour of colouring in the new signs I was drawing for Laval. Even Marie, who would not return to Titan's beloved United States, came back to work for me as did Evelyne whom we stole from Julia. The three of us were anxious to have a repeat performance of the first restaurant's success, and this time we had two great years of experience behind us. On top of that, I'd understood that complete devotion is success's most nutritious meal. I'd have to put my cook's apron back on full-time and start flipping crêpes on the Laval boulevard. We accepted the challenge with flying colours! The new restaurant was full from the first day we opened, and it was never empty again during the five years our lease would keep us in the little shopping centre.

It was exhilarating to see the customers from around the area preferring our restaurant to the neighbouring places; to see the solicitors and barristers from the buildings across the street running to our place at noon; to see the day filled with business travellers, women dressed in the latest fashions, servers from other restaurants, bailiffs, police officers, and all kinds of new brotherhoods parading through the restaurant in search of CORA'S famous breakfasts. Famous because they'd been mentioned in a big newspaper the Sunday before the Laval opening. In the February 25, 1990 edition of *La Presse*, a certain Johanne Mercier did indeed sing the praises of the blond Cora who'd opened a restaurant that served breakfast from six in the morning until three in the afternoon, seven days a week. The reporter talked about our "simple" breakfasts, which she said had more a "plastic-curtain-and-tablecloth" style than a luxury hotel style. She mentioned the "nice," though slightly "kitsch" décor, and the chickens that came from every place imaginable. She boasted about our healthy choices of fresh fruit and our chatty good humour. At the end of her article, the addresses of both restaurants were printed.

It was impossible not to recognize that Providence had come to me disguised as all kinds of strangers that I needed to know. A young letter carrier had bought my Boisbriand house; Angelo Machinpoulos had agreed to sell his restaurant to a French woman; the old civil servant at the court house had advised me to call the business *Chez Cora*; the salesman from Saint-Hyacinthe offered us the kitchen equipment of the future; a certain Johanne Mercier took charge of doing our publicity; and our friend Bob gave us free wood to renovate the new restaurant. Pablo, Fatima, Evelyne, Nicole, and even Mary E., the coffee salesman, Mr. Pom, Marcel the firefighter, and so many others were sincerely attached to us. The most amazing part was the army of invisible police officers who, morning after morning, set the traffic on a straight path to our two breakfast businesses. More than ever, I could feel the delicate pressure of the angel supporting my arm, lighting the grill before me when the morning fog was stubborn, and lifting me when I felt the awful distrust. I learned to let go, to trust love, and bless my life, despite the presence within me of a monster ego that was preparing itself to become president and first orchestra leader of a big breakfast symphony.

CHAPTER 43

The Arrival of Fresh Pork

THE ROAST PORK NEVER HAD TIME TO EXPLAIN TO US HOW IT ended up on our menu. Was it thanks to my mother in Limbo whispering to get my attention, or was it in response to the babbling of our young solicitor Chouchou who was seated at table eight of the new Saint-Martin *Chez Cora*? People were always asking for it in Laval! And Evelyne urged me not to disappoint the professional arena.

"Since the suits and ties prefer us to the pink taramasalata of the Greek delicatessens, we must," she insisted, "fill their plates and tickle their noses."

Interested in the roast, Julia arrived in Laval with the firm intention of convincing us to serve fresh pork at breakfast. She wanted to tell us her own version of what to do with the animal whose innards her grandmother in Sainte-Adèle flavoured with garlic.

One day, Julia had gone with her grandmother to

Old Man Chalifoux's on Route 10 and saw her go with the old butcher into the little white room that served as the business' refrigerator. When she came back out of the semi-darkness, Yaya had in her arms a piece of meat cut from an animal whose back fat she'd measured herself. She put the meat on a block of wood used as a table and then guided the butcher's knife until the dark pink flesh rolled up on itself, showing a thin seed of blanched lard. The butcher tied the roast and gave it back to the satisfied customer.

"You have to cook pork well because of the parasites," Yaya had insisted when she brought the roast home.

Slits were made in the rind of the roast and precious cloves of garlic (she always had a big jar on the counter next to the sink) were slipped into the thin openings. The roast had to be well-peppered and sprinkled with yellow powder which, according to her, was a fine substitute for the cheap mustard from Provigo's. Yaya would then put the meat in an old green stoneware pot, taking care to add enough water to keep the roast from drying out as it cooked. Because it had a bad habit of hardening while it was in the oven, Yaya suggested this be done at a low temperature. That would preserve the juice and tenderness of the meat.

Julia then told us about their nights in Sainte-Adèle when the smell of the roast would get their bellies rumbling. Under no circumstances would their grandmother slice the meat before it was completely cooled off. The roast would come out of the oven a little before the television news was broadcast; Yaya would pour the cooking juice into a little blue granite bowl, and, as it set, this would become the roast grease.

The next morning, in the icebox on the porch, they'd find the roast wrapped in brown butcher paper. At breakfast, Yaya would take out our old Belgian ancestor's knife and cut two slices per child, and, in addition to her own portion, keep for herself any pieces that were too tough for young teeth.

Roast pork mornings were a party in Sainte-Adèle. My mother was still making homemade bread at that time and she always made a fresh loaf to go with the roast.

***

In Laval, the notary's nose was much longer than the red curls on his little pear-shaped head. His complexion was the colour of fresh butter and his nice blue eyes looked like the ones used in the giant stuffed puppies at the Duvernay Miracle Mart. We gave him the nickname Chouchou because of a story he told us one morning when the electricity was out and he'd managed, despite the mountains of snow, to climb over the median on the boulevard to get to the last pot of hot coffee in the new snack bar. It was a story about how his own mother would cook him suckling pig roast, behind the back of his Grandpa Schiller, who'd recently retired from the Laronde Ballenstein law office. The notary was the old man's favourite despite the awful affront represented by the marriage of his father, Brian Schiller, of Westmount, to his mother, Mandoline Tremblay, of Jonquière.

Brian and Mandoline lived off the European textile importing business until they inherited four million dollars from a pioneer, who, though distant, had been the beautiful Mandoline's only rich relative. Since then, they'd lived in luxury, in a town house on Ile-Patton that they'd paid a cool million for, including parking.

As the little story's only heir, Chouchou dared to ask us for roast pork during the snow storm. He commandeered every muscle in his handsome face to get his mouth to pronounce a sublime sentence, with all the right emotion.

"Please, Miss Evelyne."

"Only in the winter," I answered, promising the gentleman that we would serve him roast pork like his mother used to make for breakfast.

"Like the Sainte-Adèle roast!" added a victorious Julia.

The very next day, Evelyne called Maurice from Délipro to order a relatively lean shoulder cut, tied and covered with a few layers of lard to keep it from drying out while it cooked. A new breakfast was about to be added to our repertoire. And of course, out of respect for my mother, we named it the SAINTE-ADÈLE.

Chouchou the notary knew hundreds of businessmen in Laval and he brought them all to our place for breakfast. He himself introduced them to the fresh roast pork dish, served with eggs or homemade beans. He bragged about how good our crusty bread was, the cleanliness of our two griddles, and the irresistible cake the boss would bring to her customers herself, at noon on weekdays.

The notary was right: I'd started making my upside-down cakes with renewed energy. The second restaurant was like a promised land for me, with more room, more people, and more dreams to make come true.

CHAPTER 44

We Are Imitated

OUR FIRST *CHEZ CORA* WAS A GOOD LITTLE MATCHMAKER who'd given us the opportunity to have a live rehearsal; but the second *Chez Cora* turned us into real artists. As if I was Céline Dion herself, I could hear our success shouted upon the lips of the stupefied suburbanites; I could see it with my own eyes and I could hear it when it knocked on my door to be let in. And, the best part was that I could still see the hand of the angel through the haze of our achievement.

For long, wonderful moments, I felt completely at one with everything in the world and, at the same time, attached to supreme kindness and its many benefits. I felt as if I was surrounded by richness, abundance and infinite possibilities.

***

The new restaurant offered us real customers every day, people who were different from the Côte-Vertu family. So many people we didn't know came to see us that it was impossible to tell our story to each of them. But it was probably this subtle detachment that finally allowed us to become real professionals.

There were so many people to serve that we didn't have time to comment on the raisins in the apple crumble, or to happily delve into a favourite customer's intimate biography. Still, no one seemed to be suffering. No one was asking for more attention, a personal smile, or the little loving words that were required for digestion at Côte-Vertu.

The customers were delighted by our food and everyone was glad to talk about us out in the world. They talked so much about us that they even came to suffer from the lack of space in the little snack bar where, apparently, the best breakfasts ever were served. Every day, on Saint-Martin Boulevard, hundreds of hungry people offered us the opportunity to sharpen our spatulas and develop our talents as magicians.

Greek restaurateurs and the clients of other well-known restaurants sat down regularly at our counter, like schoolchildren at their desks. With amazed faces, they watched the manoeuvres at the two big griddles.

It was hard for the Greeks to accept the sudden revolution that was happening right there on their home turf, in their own area of expertise. Especially since the upheaval was being caused by an unknown housewife and it was continuing here, before their own eyes, on the famous Laval boulevard that had been previously reserved for their own Olympian heroes.

But they insisted on watching and they stayed stuck to their plastic stools. They couldn't figure out how this little restaurant with its hand-drawn posters was pulling the clients away from their mahogany interiors where, like good hosts, they offered a chicken kabob for less than a plate of banana crêpes.

"That woman probably doesn't deserve all the applause she's been getting," sang one of the watchers, with poison darts in his voice. "Wasn't she married to a Greek man? Didn't she work in Dimitri's restaurant?"

The same macho guy, with his overly thick moustache, even insinuated that the wench spoke Greek and that her intelligence had probably come from rummaging around in Greek mythology.

Despite their wild imaginings, they left the restaurant with a well-learned lesson: breakfast is worth spending time on.

"A few ounces of crêpe mix and a sliced banana cost less than souvlaki meat," one of them concluded.

"All you have to do is hire some young flunky to flip eggs while the chef debones the chicken," added his associate.

"Anyway, with the new popularity of oven-baked Greek potatoes, we don't need a fryer so much anymore and could easily stuff a breakfast griddle in between two other pieces of equipment," a third continued.

With one voice, they claimed that it was urgent to win back the confused customers as quickly as possible, before they got used to going to the new snack bar.

So, on their beautiful damask tablecloths, the fellows started serving blueberry pancakes that tasted like veal cutlet Amalfitata; and soon, most of the big places on the boulevard had to open their doors before the sun even had its first cup of coffee.

The second *Chez Cora* gave us wings and we used them to outdistance the "festive" mornings the competition was now advertising, at reduced prices. The more the value of the egg decreased in their screaming ads, the more we replied by calmly placing new inventions on our clients' tables. When the restaurant owners started to become interested in the CORA phenomenon, our little team was very flattered by the implicit compliment. But when they started imitating dish after dish on their chicken, spaghetti, or kabob menus, I became even more convinced myself of the extraordinary potential of our CORA breakfasts.

CHAPTER 45

A Dream of Expansion

A FEW MONTHS AFTER THE SECOND RESTAURANT OPENED, A travelling salesman offered us free placemats where local businesses advertised their wares. The stranger stated that I could display my logo free of charge in the centre of each placemat, as long as I used them on our tables for the next six months. It was an interesting proposal, I thought to myself, as I asked the salesman if I could have both addresses under the logo.

"My, my, do you mean to tell me you have another restaurant that's as busy as this one, little lady?!" said the man in surprise.

But I wasn't listening to him; with one eye shut, I was already drawing two little houses planted on two different roads on a street map whose edges were already sporting ads for steam cleaning, dog food, Midas mufflers, ultra-safe tanning, and the latest fad in furniture stuffing. When the vice-president of Imago, Inc.

told me that would be a good idea, a third little CORA house was preparing to appear on the imaginary map. It was indeed that very day, early in April 1990, that I felt for the first time like a force outside of me was building three, five, fifteen, fifty CORA restaurants in my head as easily as if I'd drawn them myself.

And I wanted more than anything to use this new creative energy, to link it to all my ideas, all my projects, and all my dreams; I instinctively knew that these new seeds were stronger than all my other energies put together.

Since we'd managed to reproduce the Côte-Vertu craze on Saint-Martin Boulevard, it would mean that we could do it again, three, five, fifteen, fifty times, as often as we wanted.

***

Lunch time started to stretch through the chaos of late-risers devouring our egg dishes. We had to plan a second pot of soup, and, since our budget allowed it, to hire a second cook who would be solely in charge of the noon meal: a rather rare bird to try to find in the cohort of young maidens I'd been working with since starting the first *Chez Cora*. But the rare beast came of its own accord when Léna Kiriakou returned from Thessalonica. We had once worked together at Mr. Dimitri's, but she'd left the business to follow her opera singer of a husband, whom the Greek fatherland was finally going to award a pension to after ten years. Greek bureaucracy having once again lost its way, the couple had to return to Montreal. With no apartment, and almost no money, Léna would have agreed to sing herself if I'd asked her to. She had been Dimitri's title-less accountant and had shown herself to be meticulous at a time when such a thing was rare in our kind of business.

Léna quickly agreed to cook as long as she could also look after both businesses' books in the afternoon. It was incredible — the woman would serve the milkman shepherd's pie and by dessert, she'd be bargaining with him over the price of coffee cream. Léna also negotiated for the vegetables that went in the soup, accusing the turnips of absorbing salt, or blaming the cabbage for the rather unfortunate digestive situation it would cause. In one breath, she could complain about beans from Quebec being too small and U.S. eggplants being too big.

Since Léna was now looking after the books for the first two restaurants, I now had time to explore the possibility of a third CORA snack bar.

Besides that, Marie had moved permanently from Cote-Vertu and was reigning over the Saint-Martin griddle. And at Côte-Vertu, a customer was starting to talk business with Julia.

CHAPTER 46

The Family Grew

MARTINE LATOURELLE WORKED IN CUSTOMER SERVICE AT Cell Interurbain. She spent her days attached to a console with a metallic wire no wider than a piece of spaghetti. The woman had gotten tired of this sort of work a long time ago, but no opportunity had never knocked hard enough for her to open the door and let it in. She and I had often chatted, back when I would stack the fruit for the upside-down cake at Côte Vertu. Martine would watch me lay the apples in the sugar and say she was jealous of me, of how casual we could be in the snack bar, and of the warmth that came from genuine contact with customers. She wanted to cut the terrible cord that bound her to the four weeks of vacation offered by the national giant. But she didn't dare. Then I heard Julia say Martine wanted to buy the Côte Vertu restaurant.

"So she can take care of it while we keep on opening

up other ones," Julia repeated at the other end of the phone.

Martine's boyfriend had just inherited a rather large sum and he was prepared to let his beloved enjoy it. She told Tony what she wanted to do when she brought him to lunch at *Chez Cora*. I suppose that was when, just over the counter, our friendly angel cut the first slice of our future cake. Tony offered enough money to get us thinking. Since it would be unthinkable to abandon *Miss Cote Vertu* to any other life than the one we had recently breathed into her, I insisted that the snack bar's mission remain the same, along with the name, and that the food served would be identical to what we served on Saint-Martin Boulevard. Martine agreed to follow these conditions; she understood how important my request was and was ready to put her signature on an agreement to follow these early principles of the business called CORA.

***

Was it really Providence that had untied the Cell Interurban knot, and had it also pulled on the receptionist's cord until she abandoned her phone? Was it the great Manitou that had caused Tony's old Uncle Tom to choke to death in his Pointe-au-Calumet nursing home? Or was it the devil himself who had once again come to tempt me to reach beyond my grasp?

My mother would have opted for Satan and would have told me the worst was already on its way. Luckily, in my head, a helpful hand was propping up the framework of a destiny that was now taking shape. Whether I was ecstatic or imprisoned by tragic despair, I was now able, when necessary and in a fraction of a second, to call up the whole string of imaginary CORA restaurants, and shake it until, at just the right time, each one of the little houses fell out of my noggin and onto the real earth at my feet.

CHAPTER 47

Harvest 90

With the first *Chez Cora* in Martine Latourelle's capable hands, Julia arrived in Laval like a mermaid in the middle of a tornado. She'd agreed to personally borrow the ten thousand dollars it would cost to redo the restaurant, and now she felt more at home than any old sparrow flying the coop. And barely even four weeks went by before she started trying to chase the mother bird out. At Côte-Vertu, she had learned to perfectly master all the breakfast dishes and she also knew by heart all the lunch dishes that the customers clamoured for. Julia showed rather remarkable leadership in the business. When she was at the griddle, we joked it was time to ask an additional fee for the seats at the counter. Under her firm rule, the whole snack bar soon became the best place to see and be seen. On Sundays, the customers would grow younger by the hour. Early in the morning, Julia herself would bring a bowl of oatmeal to the old couples she recognized and, at around two in the afternoon, she'd throw kiwi peels at anyone who dared get to close to her magic spatula. She was able to be furious and fair within the same second, she was independent and, at the same time, she generously and pleasantly comforted anyone who needed it.

But despite many attempts, I never managed to get her to arrive at the time written on a work schedule. As much as she had a gift for exasperating me with her differences of opinion, she also delighted me with her extraordinary insight. And Julia was as changeable as the weather, as curious as an owl, and as much a gourmand as a frog before its feast of gnats.

That's how, one chilly morning in 1990, while we were trying to come up with a new breakfast to commemorate our arrival on the boulevard in Laval, Julia invented the treat that quickly came to enjoy the most success of all the dishes on our menu.

Like almost every Saturday back then, Julia arrived at work late, once again absent-minded from the wild tango she'd danced the whole night before with her friends Evelyne, Maryse, Marco, Caroline, Juan and Domingo.

To escape the double reprimand she'd get from her boss/mother, as soon as she walked in the door my daughter took refuge in a conversation with the baker who was supplying us with the famous cinnamon raisin brioche we'd recently been looking for. Julia grabbed one of the big brioche, squeezed it and decided to slice it through the middle. She then dunked the two halves in the spiced French toast batter and gently laid them on the griddle. The pieces of bread shivered in fear, but little by little they gave in to the fiery kisses and were transformed into a surprising treat. Just when Julia was lifting the two golden pieces of brioche to place them on a big white plate, inspiration gave my daughter a little push. It made her eyes sparkle so brightly that even Mr. Leboeuf, our new Laval baker, understood that Julia had just had a brilliant idea. Then she placed a sunny side up egg and two slices of bacon on one side of the golden brioche and decorated the other half of the plate with a big mountain of fresh fruit.

"There you go, Mother, there's your Saint-Martin special!"

"Bravo, Julia! That's a wonderful harvest that's come from all the seeds I've been planting in your head!"

And that's where we got the name for the dish: HARVEST 90. The new invention was applauded by everyone who was there. It was immediately offered to the regulars, and in a few days it became the uncontested star of the drawings that hung on our walls.

***

Intoxicated by the popularity her recent discovery had

earned her, Julia insisted that we print a real menu; a menu that meant the customers didn't have to crane their necks as they scanned the walls for what they wanted to eat. A menu that, above all, would explain in detail the composition of the delicious HARVEST 90, emphasizing that the dish had been invented by none other than Julia herself.

Because Martine Latourelle was getting used to our Côte-Vertu orphans and because an old work friend was exhausting herself selling houses in the Lower Laurentians, I would again have the opportunity to search for the next location.

CHAPTER 48

The Third Cora

Julia got along wonderfully with Léna and considered her a real aunt who had come to live with us. Since she'd arrived, the shepherd's pie had also discovered a long lost relative hiding in the pan of moussaka. Of course, eggplant replaced the pearly niblets of corn over the layer of meat, but the architecture was the same, and the customers demanded almost as much. Lentils and chick peas were floating in our soups, slices of zucchini occasionally accompanied the meatballs, and a delicious garlicky white sauce sometimes replaced the barbecue sauce in the chicken dish at noon. Lemon syrup moistened the vanilla cake and the rice pudding was starting to become a topic of conversation. Strangely, the imported flavours, which had disappeared with my husband and more than ten years of trouble, returned with Aunt Léna and stuck to the family as if they'd never gone away. The customers adored the mix of aromas and borrowed words.

Julia had the strange habit of never giving up until she got something. It was probably her way of giving orders. For several days, she tried to convince Léna to work Saturday and Sunday, and to take Monday and Tuesday off.

"On the weekend, the only thing that will increase the number of dollars in the cash register would be sharper management of the line-up and the way the tables are turned over," declared my daughter, playing professor of management. And Auntie Léna was the only one who could do it, she declared, proud of her best argument yet in convincing the ambitious accountant.

Without knowing it, Julia had just caught two birds with the same idea. She'd also removed the final hesitation I had about leaving the snack bar. I was going to design a real menu, and then I could go back to pounding the pavement looking for the parking lot CORA's third little house would land next to.

The perspective of expansion set me on fire. The May weather was beautiful, and I asked Ishmaël, the Saint-Martin dishwasher, to set up a table outside in one of the shopping centre's paved corridors, where the sun managed to shine. At Omer DeSerres', I bought some pencils and bevel-tipped markers that I planned to use to immortalise our famous breakfasts.

I'd just drawn a bird on the peak of a big *J*, when a strange smell of exotic spices filtered into my nose. A certain Martha Giroux had left her stool at the counter after bathing her tonsils in several cups of black coffee. Impatient, she crossed through the private part of the snack bar and was now blocking the sun, perched on stilts that were almost as red as hell fire.

***

Martha Giroux had been the successful manager of a kebab restaurant. She had a natural talent for service and boasted that she knew everything about a working man's life. Martha had been placed in a boarding school at the age of three by the only parent she'd ever known. After Martha left the institution, and to keep the little girl from crying and following her, her mother had the idea of sitting her on top of the high balustrade of a long staircase that turned back on itself at the bottom. Perched in a seated position, the little girl quickly understood that she was the only one who could guide her unusual planet and, because of that, she'd grown up strong and determined. As a young adult, she'd made friends with what was good and put up with evil, like any good soldier would in his trench. Martha later married a rich man from Baie-d'Urfé. Then, just after she'd mastered every aspect of conjugal compromise, she gave up its benefits to another woman. She went back to work to run Mr. Dimitri's kebob place, where I met her for the first time in 1980. In 1982, when a terrible car accident almost put an end to her professional career, Martha persisted in moving her limbs in therapeutic baths until she could again hold her head as high as everyone else. She pushed herself and ultimately got her real estate license, which allowed her to work from home at her own pace.

Then, as time went by and the cruel winter began to cover the terraces of her properties, she became disillusioned. Her clients celebrated Christmas and waited for spring by paying back what they owed. And when the pretty buds began to precede the leaves on trees, an army of newly-licensed realtors started criss-crossing the suburbs in search of clients. When she finally convinced a homeowner to trust the sale of his shelter to her, Martha had to transport heavy signs and plant them herself in the still half-frozen ground in front of the bungalow. She had to move fast. When she found potential buyers, Martha would spend considerable time driving them around, but often they'd decide to sign with a competitive agent. But our Martha went on, inventing her own motivational campaigns. She could act like she was the only real estate agent on the continent. By encouraging couples who were selling and reassuring those who were buying, she managed to come through the real estate crisis of late 1990 in pretty good shape.

But fighting tired her out. And it was her brutal loss of energy that reminded her I existed. That I'd managed to recover from my burnout and that my spatula and I weren't having too much trouble making it through the recession. In her childhood, Martha had understood that analysis meant paralysis and that you have to shift directions when misery starts hitting your windshield. In her head, she had it all planned out before she even opened her mouth to say, "What are you drawing there, old friend?"

"Martha! It's been a long time! How are you?"

"You drawing a menu? I hope you're not going to take the posters down off the walls."

"What have you been up to all this time, Martha? What about real estate?"

"Hmph! Don't even talk about it, it's over!"

Then she looked more intently at the little bird with the half open beak that was half drawn on the paper.

"That kind of writing is rare. I see you've drawn three houses at the bottom of the middle page. Are you up to something I don't know about?"

"It's just visualisation, but, yeah, I'd like to open a third restaurant."

"Well, I know where you're going to do it! Here, write this address under the third house: 19831 Laurentides Boulevard, in Vimont."

"What are you talking about, Martha? That street is right next to Saint-Martin."

"Not that close and what I'm suggesting is a restaurant where all you'll have to do is paint and bring in your things. It's a Greek kebob restaurant that just closed. We could do it together, you and I."

"Martha, what are you talking about?"

"Do you want your third house or not?"

"Yes!"

And again, that awful word fell from my mouth and began to hop about across the half-drawn menu. I could see it swimming in the whiteness of the paper between "Bowl of Corn Flakes" and the SURPRISE breakfast. Then, suddenly, it hid between behind a piece of ham. The YES marched up and down around my inventions like a temperamental child I couldn't satisfy; it wanted more and more, and its rash parade made me agree to go and see the place where it might just become real.

"Maybe it would be a good idea to go see this restaurant."

"Absolutely, but I'm warning you, if you decide to buy it, I'm your partner!"

"Martha! Please, give me time to think!"

"Analysis means paralysis, remember that while you're thinking!"

And with those words, Martha disappeared. I still had to draw the crêpe page, but it wasn't enough to satisfy the YES. And I heard myself whisper, "Yes, yes! One of these days we'll have to visit that abandoned kebob place."

CHAPTER 49

An Old Sultan

IN THE MEANTIME, SULTAN RAGMAN REAPPEARED IN MY LIFE. As a friend, of course; because a man like Macrabi never allowed himself to swim in waters that were as familiar as the snack bar. He'd call me from time to time, at night, and we'd spend long hours talking about the magnificent dreams I was trying to slip into his cold imagination.

"Cora! Be realistic," he insisted. "You've been lucky up to now and you have to be careful. You can't think about travelling around the world when you're just learning how to ride a bike. You have to understand that your ideas are too big for your means. You're making a living! Thank God now and be happy that you have the chance to offer work to your own children! You don't know the real business world. You still don't know that it's not a good thing to be too ambitious."

I could hear Macrabi's exasperated voice echoing

from the phone. He was the first maharaja after my husband's time to knock on my door, and we dated for a while. Then one day a little bug got into his ear or maybe an angel disguised as a vocal cord shouted from the depths of his strange Lebanese heart — "Roll up your sleeves, my girl, and work to earn a living. I'm certainly not going to put a new ring on your finger!"

With that, despite all the future benefits that would come from his sublime declaration, the dragon's fiery breath reduced my feminine naïveté to ashes.

Macrabi witnessed my burnout from the distance of his lace empire. In his own way he'd worried about me. Once he'd even slipped me a few dollars, discreetly hidden between the tumultuous pages of Michel Tremblay's *The Heart Laid Bare*. Then we spaced out the times we got together until we didn't know when we'd see each other again. Obeying his stinging recommendation, I'd rolled up my sleeves to open the first *Chez Cora* and, two years later, a second one.

At the end of the phone line, Macrabi was talking to a zombie. He was urging me to give up the idea of opening a third restaurant, and I was dreaming about what colour the next day's noodle soup would be.

Sometimes, without him knowing, one of his reprimands would succeed in waking me up. I'd come to with a start, with fear at my heels and the sultan's curse locked up in my head. I had no intention of trying anything at all; I could see myself, sitting on a dirty bench in Saint-Louis Square, trying to pull a rhyme from the face of a shrub that had been half devoured by despair. I'd toss and turn in my bed, my eyes wide open because none of my dreams wanted to have anything to do with such worry. Those mornings, I'd arrive at the snack bar in an awful state. When she would see me, Léna would immediately ask me to leave again. She'd pretend we were short on grapefruit or crusty cinnamon bread. She'd send me as far away as possible, to give my guardian angel time to wake up too.

Then, the Invisible Arm would grab my neck and squeeze so tightly with its elbow that it felt like an attempt to remove evil; to push it out through my mouth, my ears and each eye socket, which the recent nightmare had decorated with a red halo. Then I'd return to the snack bar with five kilos of oranges or a case of kiwis, although we already had plenty. Those occasions were never useless to my children, because when I was suffering like that the poor kids would have bought me the moon if they thought it would make me feel better.

***

Freed from my fears, I once again took up the torch of our future. My third restaurant wasn't born from nothing, it appeared in my head, spit from a creative lightening bolt that just happened to be in there. And I was convinced that its perfect form already existed, hidden in the shade of a birch tree. Even though I came from humble beginnings, as the sultan reminded me so eloquently, it did no good to judge a book by its cover. So, a few days after I started to draw our first menu, the whole team and I went to visit what would become the third Cora address.

CHAPTER 50

Spiros Christakakis

THE *DELICE DE VIMONT* DIDN'T LOOK LIKE ANYTHING MY imagination ever could have come up with. It was a mass of serviceable outgrowths that had destroyed the initial structure of a little dairy shop at the origin of the remodelling frenzies undertaken by three different owners.

The building had been purchased, three years before, by a certain Spiros Christakakis. He'd turned it into a kebab restaurant by setting up a fifty-two seat windowed terrace at beginning of the series of additions. He'd cheated his own parking lot to do it, but "It's better to have fifty customers inside the restaurant than cars in the parking lot," the Greek brain had concluded.

The kebab restaurant had been purchased to assure the future of Christakakis's twin boys. The whole inside was covered with sheets of dark brown panelling and real oak had been used for the frames of the Corfu-blue vinyl booths.

When they stepped inside this palace, Julia and Evelyne immediately felt sick!

“Never, Mother! We’ll never be able to transform this into a CORA!” declared my daughter.

“Hold on, little one,” replied Léna, “you have to have a bit of imagination! Let your mother have a look around the place.”

I walked through the restaurant trying to ignore the thirty plastic vines that were tumbling over the tables. It was awful. We’d have to repaint it all, remove the artificial plants, add a few fake windows to the back wall, change the fabric on the booths, sew little valances for the terrace, add a few stations for clearing the dirty dishes, transform the bar into a fruit counter, and maybe hang a collection of old sieves or cooking utensils over it. We’d also undoubtedly have to install a few trellises here and there to make some cosy spots, decorate the wide window ledges in the entry, and paper the walls and the washrooms like we had on Saint-Martin.

“Nothing we can’t do with what we have right now,” I thought out loud.

Of course the kitchen would need a good steam cleaning, but it just so happened that a new business owner was boasting about that very thing on our advertising placemats. And we’d have to buy three Miraclean griddles in order to serve the 160 customers the restaurant could hold.

"Are you crazy, Mom? We run a snack bar, not a Chinese buffet!"

"We have a breakfast place, sweetie! We'll just need more people on the griddle on Sundays."

Léna agreed and she'd already figured out that if we turned the tables over three times on Sundays, we could easily serve more than 500 customers.

"Yay! Léna! I'll be in charge of the griddle," Evelyne stated. "I like when it's busy."

"You're right, Evelyne. We can serve six or seven hundred customers between the two of us with one hand tied behind our backs," added Julia, closing the discussion on the location.

Spiros Christakakis didn't know he should take us seriously until I asked him a series of questions. "How much are you asking? What about the down payment? What's the time frame on the balance? And what about rent?"

The old Greek man couldn't think that fast. Instead, he started to ramble to Léna, his fellow islander, about the hard times he'd had in his life. Then, when he saw that the sun was growing dim on the other side of the bay window on his luxurious terrace, he shortened his story, swearing to Léna that he'd made a good living in a shopping centre pizzeria in Duvernay until Anthony and Costa both decided to drop out of the college in their last year. His sons had convinced him, in

1985, that the future of Montreal's Greek colony was in kebab restaurants.

Personally, I was convinced that our own future depended on the way I presented the new opportunity to Marie Giroux.

CHAPTER 51

Becoming a Founder

As I thought it over, I came to understand that I was the founder of *Chez Cora*, and its only mother. Like a real mother, I was the one who'd heard its first cry coming from behind a sign that said *Restaurant for Sale*. I was the one who'd made all the decisions about it: like getting rid of the club sandwich and its friend the steamed hot dog and all the fried items, and exchanging all its old cooking paraphernalia for a nice big griddle. I was also the one who'd rushed to the snack bar in the pre-dawn fog, the one who'd stood up to the critics, and who'd defied the sultan's predictions about it. *Chez Cora* had marinated in my own noggin, its buds had bloomed in my head and the restaurant had come out of me like a real child. On top of that, I was surrounded by angels that I adored and could no longer do without. It was clear to me that I couldn't give up my precious baby and, despite all his wisdom,

King Solomon would be ill-advised to come and cut such a fascinating creature in two.

Chez Cora had swum in its amniotic fluid for a long time. All the mornings I'd spent *Chez Rose* came back to me; those long mornings spent writing hadn't been without a purpose — they'd contributed to the growth of the phenomenon that was now blooming right before my very eyes. And I had the right, and the responsibility, to keep it for myself.

***

I once read that a certain Dr. Kellogg invented his famous cereal in 1894 after an old woman, for whom he'd prescribed dry crackers, had broken a tooth. The doctor had to pay his client ten dollars, and he'd dreamed of creating a flakey food made from corn. The next morning, he played with boiling wheat and cut up the resulting purée until, when they were baked in the oven, the wheat shavings turned into the world's first breakfast cereal.

"The further the fisherman goes from the shore," Grandad Frédéric would say, "the bigger his cod will be."

You have to swim in deep water if you want to catch the big fish. You have to jump in if you want to learn to swim, leave the comfortable shore of what you've already done, and dare to try something different. I had to forget the fact that I had very little experience and move forward like the ice-cutting ships, breaking a path to the future as I went. And there was also that awful desire to please people, to bring them joy along with a jar of jam, or a marvellous surprise wrapped up in a crêpe, or true happiness in a little bowl of nicely cut fresh fruit. I dreamed about comfortable restaurants where the customers would feel at home; restaurants where, like at Côte-Vertu, it would be common to recognize everyone and make them feel safe by offering plenty of food. I also dreamed about treats, an occasional bouquet of flowers, ground cherries – just to surprise people — a nice piece of fudge for everyone, familiar hellos and personal attention. I wanted our customers to be completely fulfilled, to appreciate us, and to want to come back as soon as possible. I insisted on drawing our menus on the walls because I also wanted to awaken the sleeping child that was so often hiding inside each one of us; I wanted to tame each little cherub and communicate to them the joy I felt in making them happy. I wanted my food to honour the joy of living rather than the fear of dying. I wanted our customers to enjoy moments filled with richness and abundance. I especially wanted *Chez Cora* to come completely out of my head with all the courage necessary for it to reach its full potential.

***

I had to explain to Martha Giroux that certain principles had to be respected in the third *Chez Cora*; and I also had to explain that, just like in the first two *Chez Cora's*, I was the one who owned the *idea* and therefore we could never be equals in the direction the future business would take or the division of its stock shares.

Martha came to see what was going on a few days after we'd visited Christakakis's place. She'd heard that a young Chinese family had tried to buy the place from him, but the deal had fallen through at the last minute because of Grandfather Tchu. The day the contract was to be signed, they had brought the old man to the restaurant and he'd noticed that a street cut through the boulevard right where the desired property was located. In traditional Asian culture, this was a very bad sign for the future success of a business.

I'd immediately thought that, with the Chinese family out of the picture, the seller would have no choice but to accept our conditions, since none of his fellow Greeks would agree to buy a closed restaurant.

Martha had painted her false fingernails navy blue the day she'd showed up at the Saint-Martin counter. She was ready to accept anything to get out of real estate hell. She had no trouble understanding that the CORA system held market value and that I would want to be the majority shareholder of the new business.

After a few calculations, we realized that even at the lowest possible price, the purchase and renovation of the kebab restaurant would require more money than we had between the two of us. Even if Chistakakis accepted a big balance spread out over five years, we'd have to repaint everything, buy three brand new Miraclean griddles and replace all the kitchen counters with high-quality stainless steel. We'd undoubtedly need a third contribution to renovate the place.

"Cora, do you think the banks could lend us something?"

"No need, girls. I'll go in with you right now!" said a carpet-cleaner customer with sensitive ears.

"A third, a third, and a third, and Cora's third is her concept," continued the customer we knew as Robert Saint-Onge.

Martha raised her left eyebrow for an instant. Then, out of fear of paralysis, she agreed to listen to the stranger's proposal.

"We'll draw up a shareholders' agreement and it will be a done deal!" he declared, sitting down on the stool next to Martha. "I'm used to being in business and I'll show you myself how to get ahead!" he added, before I even had time to open my mouth.

"Shall we get together tonight to talk about the project and get to know each other better?" Martha suggested.

"Okay. Hmm. Can I invite you to dinner at the Pirate de Laval?" Saint-Onge asked, as his mouth changed into a little Saint Valentine's Day heart.

Robert's casual tango was going a little too fast for

my taste. But something told me that, despite my wise reflections about stock ownership, it would be a good idea to see where he planned to go. In my head, CORA's third little house was already puffing out its chest and stretching in all directions, letting me know it was ready to come out of its cocoon.

Saint-Onge's mentality was quite different from my own — he was the kind of man who would jump right into a pool with all his clothes on. He talked without really thinking and made abundant use of a kind of irresistible smile that transformed his monkey-like face into a papal benediction. We agreed, as we ate noodles at the Pirate, that I would train Robert in the kitchen while Martha looked after welcoming the customers and managed the wait staff. After a few weeks, I'd be able to step away from the restaurant to look after a fourth *Chez Cora*. (Hmm...) It was a deal!

Unfortunately, he showed up to the opening in a silk shirt. Laughing, he then told us that he hadn't bought himself a job, but a real business, and that we could forget about seeing him flipping crêpes at the griddle.

Since the famous shareholders' agreement hadn't yet been signed, and since the money he was supposed to contribute still hadn't been transferred to the new company's business account, I simply invited him to step back from our little trio. The kind of business we were running didn't need a ribbon cutter in a brocade suit, and we couldn't care less about his "real" business sense, which was already starting to look like a bunch of promises that wouldn't be kept.

"You have to solve your problems as they come up," Granddad Frédéric used to say. "Otherwise, they end up getting bigger than our ability to face them. And, you can never believe a violin salesman's promises," he would add.

"Still, some manage to make their way all across the peninsula with a single song," Mother would whisper to contradict him.

The impending sale of the Côte-Vertu restaurant put me in a position to replace Saint-Onge's contribution myself, and I ended up with his share of stock as well as my own. The fast talker's desertion was undoubtedly the hand of Providence making sure our family remained the owner of the concept! And with the opening of the new *Chez Cora* in Vimont, my son Nicholas officially began his career as our fruiter, working in a white coat at a magnificent fruit counter.

The Chinese superstition worked to our benefit. From the first week on, the place was flooded with customers. This *Chez Cora* was succeeding far beyond the realm of a snack bar. We'd set up in a place that was much bigger, a real restaurant with booths and a fruit counter that was separate from the serving counter. And it was triumphantly holding its own.

I had the feeling an angel had placed its booth right in the middle of Laurentides Boulevard, opposite the restaurant, and the same winged creature was slowing down traffic so the people in the cars could admire the beautiful building with lace in its three windows. Seeing the morning passengers turn towards the restaurant, it was easy to imagine a beneficient presence supplying them with little capsules containing the aroma of cinnamon *brioche*. Some winged strategist also sprinkled the sidewalk with little crumbs of caramelized sugar, and the cars got caught in the pleasant trap, turning quickly and slipping into our parking lot as if by magic.

CHAPTER 52

DÉLICE DE VIMONT

THE DÉLICE DE VIMONT BREAKFAST SAW THE LIGHT OF DAY a few months after the third *Chez Cora* opened, in honour of the glorious apple season, and also, naturally, to keep alive the memory of Mr. Christakakis's kebab place.

Fresh-picked fall apples have a taste like none other and the ones from Vimont had an aroma that was particularly troubling for our associate, Martha.

"Nicholas! You have to invent something for these wonderful apples. My mouth waters when I just walk by them!" Martha meowed, her red lips pulled up to her cheekbones by the torture.

And Nicholas, who always saw beyond the immediate request, added pears and fresh seedless grapes to the apples. He arranged the little cubes of fruit and cereal and then, to everyone's great surprise, he suddenly turned away from his masterpiece and climbed up to the attic through the only hatch (which happened to be situated just above his fruit counter). Martha started to reassure the customers about the fire they thought had broken out on the upper floor, when Nicholas came back down, dishevelled and carrying on his shoulder a strange box of mismatched glassware. After a few moments of suspense Nicholas poured his apple mixture into a beautiful, transparent sundae dish; he'd remembered it because he'd put it away in the attic himself with the rest of the Greek's unusable items. Martha then paraded the new breakfast through the restaurant, proud as a peacock.

In the days following, like a real magpie, she boasted about the young fruiter's talents, explaining how it only took Nicholas a few minutes to slice a big sieve full of fresh grapes in two.

"Let me teach you something this morning, my friend." Taking two covers from the little jam pot, Nicholas placed grapes in one, covering them with the other cover. Then he ran a big knife between them and *voilà*! Thirty grapes were cut with one sweep of his knife.

"Otherwise, we wouldn't have enough to serve," the head waitress added. "On Sundays, there are more people here than in the neighbourhood church!"

The DELICE DE VIMONT fruit cup would later be served in a new bowl, which was wider, deeper, and more generous. It would be served with a nicely toasted English muffin and a big portion of honey.

CHAPTER 53

The Magic Dish

In Vimont, we were amazed when we saw the customers fill up the parking lot like fish in a miraculous net. The incredible crowds were such stimulation for our creative sides that Martha's most frivolous desire was immediately transformed into a gastronomic surprise.

A little before Christmas, when our high-heeled maitre-d' was sitting and visiting on the terrace with her ex-husband, Martha called to me like Princess Diana through the clicking of cameras.

"Cora! Come meet Saul, my dear husband! And while we're at it, will you make me a surprise? I didn't eat last night and I'm so hungry I'm digesting my stomach lining."

"Martha, I'm in the middle of scrubbing the pot for the lunch meatballs. I don't have time to make up a new breakfast!"

Martha's look slid along between the dishes listed

in the morning, but nothing managed to grab her attention. Her head wanted fruit and her stomach wanted a cream- filled orgy.

I loved Martha's appetites, the way she got so excited but never sat too long in the same spot. When I got to the fruit counter, I filled a bowl with a mixture of fresh fruit. I covered it with a layer of slightly diluted pastry cream, and then built a spectacular dome with other cut fruit. The bowl looked like a springtime bouquet, but I knew only too well that beauty would not be enough to satisfy Martha's culinary request. I opted for a nicely toasted bagel, which I put through the rotary toaster twice (as she always required). Then I added a generous helping of cream cheese on the clear plate, at the foot of the bowl.

The fruit structure didn't have time to make it all the way to the terrace before a customer exclaimed, "It's magic! Tell Cora her hands are magic!"

It was magic indeed and Miss Martha got to her feet to applaud the new treat as it was set down on her table! Martha was determined not to allow a name as old as her own to be used to name the invention. Her ex-husband then suggested we call it the MAGIC breakfast.

CHAPTER 54

The Meaning of Property

At about the same time, a strange winged creature allowed a certain Camille Labonté to find her way to the centre of our organisation. Mrs. Labonté also wanted to "make a Cora" with me. She had reigned as a restaurant manager all her life and wanted to try this new formula which would also allow her to enjoy life. In order for her to learn about the way we did things and so that we could get to know her a little better, I invited her to work with us until we found a fourth site. Delighted by the offer, Mrs. Labonté worked for a few months waiting tables and in the kitchen until the day she announced that she no longer needed our help to open her own breakfast restaurant. She'd found a site I hadn't agreed with and she'd decided to go ahead and open the restaurant without me. A heavy, leaden cloud fell on my head. We'd just taught her all our recipes and now she was going to use them to compete against us.

Which beautiful angel had let me make such a stupid mistake, the worst ever really?

Once my emotions had settled, the incident turned out to be the most useful mistake I could have made. It gave us the idea of transforming the basement of the Saint-Martin restaurant into a prep kitchen where all our exclusive recipes would be made.

In its own way, the angel had taught me the value of property. It made me understand what our recipes were worth and the responsibility that fell to me to protect them. To continue in business, we'd have to look after our recipes and not leave them lying around where they could be picked up by just anyone.

Mrs. Labonté's insult gave me a lot to think about. It made me realize, once again, the extraordinary value of CORA breakfasts, a recipe that united all the recipes, a concept that was worthy of being copied down to the last detail.

Léna complained, too, about the sneaky woman. Then she got busy turning the Saint-Martin basement into a workshop kitchen. She set up a little plywood desk between the sacks of flour where she'd sit and take the orders from our three restaurants.

The volume of business was on the rise and the title-less accountant was spending whole days in the thick clouds rising from beaten sacks of flour. Léna put up with her relative misery by preaching that it was now time to start saving for the fourth *Chez Cora* which, according to her opera singer of a husband, would ultimately engulf his beloved wife completely.

CHAPTER 55

A Triumph in Vimont

In 1991 it seemed that the whole of the island of Montreal was running to the Vimont Cora. The news spread that the mother hen of the Côte-Vertu snack bar had a huge restaurant outside of town and that there was room for everyone.

In Laval, it seemed as if the restaurant industry was going through its greatest revolution since the arrival of Caesar salad on Saint-Martin Boulevard. Several neighbourhood restaurant owners came to see with their own eyes the change that had occurred in the ex-kebab restaurant. It was unimaginable — the 160-seat restaurant was full to capacity every day, and no professional logic could explain our success. With eggs, crêpes, and every kind of non-fried typical Quebec lunch, *Chez Cora* was pulling the rug out from under the white tablecloth businesses. They may have tried to copy the formula on the boulevard, but they never had the same indefinable naiveté that the scribbles on the walls helped to promote.

Some gossips predicted that Mother Cora would be impossible to replace; others said that as soon as she was out the door, the mother hen would see the sky fall on the heads of her chicks. However on Côte-Vertu, on Saint-Martin, and in Vimont, Martine Latourelle, young Julia, and Martha Giroux were managing to do the work quite well. They followed the CORA method to the letter, and respected the established rules; the food was delivered to them every day from a central kitchen, and on Sundays each restaurant's books were forwarded to Léna's floury office.

Martha Giroux was happy that Robert Saint-Onge had been asked to leave the group, because she preferred to be alone with me. She was delighted by her new adventure, and she never worried about anything because she was convinced that when you do something you like, it always works. She admitted she was fascinated by the unusual way I went about the restaurant business.

"It's like nothing I've seen in twenty years!" she said.

And my "way" included doing free-hand drawings on the walls, hanging up old olive oil cans with daisies in them, suspending spaghetti colanders above the customers' heads, and never being able to say no to anything they wanted. It meant treating employees like my own children, and leaving nothing to chance by listening to absolutely everything. It meant thinking a cardboard bird's yellow beak was as important as some rascal's blue eyes; it meant paying attention to a deliveryman's exasperated sigh and Martha's pout, which she usually hid behind a surprised exclamation.

My associate was delighted. For her, *Chez Cora* was a dazzling sight. She found every detail attractive, like the white rabbits on the clothes line strung across the terrace or the teddy bear hiding in a big, empty Oreo cookie box. She would never question the relevance of any of my inventions because she thought every single one of them was charming.

Since the place had a knack for attracting crowds, Martha was jubilant. How wonderful it was that all these people were coming to see her without her having to go find them, and without her having to plant heavy signs — the only effort she had to put forward was to be happy to welcome them. All these people, as they came in search of the famous crêpe dish, discovered the queen of the estate and got to know her and to love her. Other people's love was what Martha was looking for in this adventure, and *Chez Cora* provided her ample opportunity to do so throughout all the years she spent there.

CHAPTER 56

Dolorès Sandwich

One Saturday morning, in Vimont, an emergency room specialist from la Cité Hospital asked his friend Martha for "something besides breakfast."

"Yesterday's soup, and some kind of sandwich, anything!" shouted the boss through the kitchen door.

I didn't think the leftover elbow macaroni in the fridge would be appropriate for such a useful person. Luckily, a few hard-cooked eggs (marked with a big C, like Aunt Olivette used to do) immediately stimulated my imagination. In nothing flat, a big egg salad sandwich arose under my knife blade. Each piece of the sandwich had to be properly placed on the glass plate, so that the customer's approval would fall on the garnish first.

When it was served, with a few pieces of seasonal fruit, the dish was worthy of being recorded in history. Since everyone knew I hated sickness, it was out of the question to think of giving the sandwich the name of a hospital. The new creation rambled around for a while without a name, until the day when Martha's mother came to the restaurant for the first time.

Dolorès had taken advantage of a trip to Trois-Rivières to continue along Highway 40 all the way to Laval. Creeping down the new CORA's long entryway, the sixty-year-old wanted to surprise Martha.

"Hey there! It's me, Mom! Hi there, sweetie."

"Mom!" Martha exclaimed, sniffing at her mother's garlicky profile. "Mom, it's really you! Come, I'll show you around my new restaurant!"

The visit took two long hours, as Martha and her mother caught up on the ten months of back news that the new business had unfortunately inserted between mother and daughter.

"Martha," Mother Dolorès suddenly exclaimed, "why isn't your name written on the menu?"

Martha didn't have the heart to tell her she hated her name and that the worst thing of all would be to see it on the menu every day.

"Because we were waiting for you so we could use your name instead of mine; just to make you happy, Mother dear."

When the honour fell upon the sixty-year-old's shoulders, her body sank down into the booth's plastic seat. In a few seconds, her creamy white face turned raspberry red. CORA's magic wand had struck again.

The egg salad sandwich was immediately named DOLORÈS NOON. The blossoming of Dolorès' happiness is a sound that still rings in my ears.

CHAPTER 57

The First Menu

I'D DRAWN A FANCIFUL BLUE MENU FOR JULIA ON A BIG white sheet of paper folded in three like a big *Z* that had pulled its two branches in towards its trunk. It was our first menu and our customers loved it, despite the occasional black inky mess caused by the words running into each other.

"Yum, yum!" exclaimed everyone when they saw the new Quatro crêpes with four kinds of fruit and smelled the aromas arising from the batter for potbellied *crespelles*.[4]

Julia was also very happy because the story of the origin of her HARVEST 90 breakfast was longer than any other on the whole menu. I even dared to invent the word *paindoréssimo* to describe our French toast made from two thick slices of *brioche* dipped in vanilla-flavoured egg batter. A little later, Madame Labonté had the nerve to use the same made-up word to describe her own French toast.

[4] Tiny *crêpes*.

The new menu came into use in all three CORA restaurants at once. The day before M-Day, we got all the employees of the three locations together at Saint-Martin so we could explain it to them, and we used our spatulas to show them all the new items and the necessary adjustments. That same night, all the signs on the walls of the three CORA snack bars would have the price of each breakfast removed. I drew many little black stripped bees and turquoise butterflies that we placed over the holes left by the staples when they were removed with the price lists. In this way, from one day to the next, without anyone really noticing, a cloud of bees and butterflies increased the number of dollars in the three restaurants' tills by more than five per cent. The number of customers, along with the number of satisfied sighs, also increased. Everyone was talking about the mice drawn in the cheese, about the old-fashioned porridge, and about the three sausages wrapped in cheddar cheese and hidden inside buckwheat crêpes. They noticed the BREAKFAST 88, APRIL 89, and HARVEST 90 breakfasts. And that allowed many of them to realize that Mother Cora was showing some connection between her ideas.

"Wow!" exclaimed one stranger. "The owner was nice enough to thank her suppliers!"

I also drew three little houses next to the addresses of the three CORA restaurants. Beneath them, I placed an empty nest waiting for its new batch of eggs. The message got through loud and clear.

CHAPTER 58

Peter Papathanassopoulos

THAT MESSAGE HAD BEEN REPEATING AND REPEATING IN MY head ever since I started browning pieces of French toast in the Vimont kitchen. We hadn't managed to inject quite enough vanilla into the carpet cleaner's blood to make a cook out of him; therefore I'd been on watch over the pots and pans while Martha looked after the flow of customers.

On Saint-Martin, Léna kept droning on and on about the atomic seed that had already split three times since the beginning!

"Blahblahblah!" I would repeat back to her, refusing to admit there were any obstacles.

Also, on the subject of seeds, five years later I read a wonderful sentence that has remained engraved in my memory: "It's always possible to count the number of seeds in an apple, but it's impossible to count the number of apples in a seed." Later on I came to understand that my seed was as tough as it was because it contained an entire orchard!

We still needed new recruits because a slow Monday in Vimont was the same as a Sunday on Côte-Vertu. Besides the thousands of unbudgeted dollars for Léna, the constant patronage brought with it a bit of worry for the entrepreneur I was becoming. How the hell could I plan a fourth CORA when I had the awful obligation of serving over three hundred breakfasts every weekday morning in Vimont? We'd managed to catch the eye of three new cooks, but at the last minute, they opted for Pacini, or a position in a brewery, or the Kraft cafeteria in Saint-Laurent. Since we served three times more meals in an hour than a normal commercial kitchen, we decided we'd have to increase the hourly wage; we couldn't treat our employees as if they were preparing two kebabs every half hour. We'd also have to be five or ten times nicer than any other employer in order to give a good cook a reason to put up with the constant commotion and to prefer working for us to working somewhere else.

The angel refined our understanding of human resources; it planted the first seeds in the very heart of the euphoric abundance of the early months in Vimont, and plotted to keep me in the centre of our hiring difficulties. How could I dream about my string of little houses when I didn't have competent personnel? I couldn't be everywhere at once. And I refused to give up on the idea. I'd have to find solutions.

"A kitchen training program," suggested young Nicholas. "We have to plan a restaurant as a completely autonomous unit, with no Mother Cora at the griddle, no Evelyne, or Marie, or Julia, or Léna anywhere."

"We have to imagine a complete team that will be able to work by applying our way of doing business," Julia, the seasoned manager, added.

This challenge became the urgent task of the day. However, the angel decided it was time to get moving despite the fact that our ideas were only half-ripe. It whispered into the ear of a certain Papathanassopoulos that there was a person who could probably get him out of a tight spot.

Despite the fact that he was five months behind on his rent, despite the fact that the bank was starting to raise its voice, and despite the fact that his customers were jumping ship, Peter Papathanassopoulos still hoped to find someone to buy his 2800-square foot delicatessen on Labelle Boulevard in Chomedy.

It was a nice restaurant with an open kitchen and oak booths that had been built only two years earlier, but it had never really become a hit with the public. It's not unusual for magnificent places to open their doors, only to border on bankruptcy a few months later because they're lacking something that's not always easy to put your finger on. On top of that, the Chomdedy restaurant was tragically lacking in family support. Since its birth, it had been tossed back and forth from cousin to cousin, and not a single shareholder had a strong enough back to take on the legal guarantees. The business's survival had come to depend solely on the tolerance of the leaseholders who were looking at their shopping centre's fourth business closing.

The angel whispered into Peter's ear that right there, in Laval, a group of women had just managed to revive Christakakis's kebab place and that, if he stretched his neck enough, he'd be able to see the big yellow sun and its overflowing parking lot.

***

Peter Papathanassopoulos had taken on the role of *pater familias* when he'd arrived in Canada in 1959. He'd washed those near death at the Jewish General Hospital for five years before he became the smoked-meat slicer at the famous Bob's Deli in downtown Montreal. A certain Mr. Shear had noticed Peter's delicate touch when he'd lifted poor Cousin Jacob's side. Unable to communicate with the stranger, Mr. Shear had given him his business card to thank him. Marvin Shear was the delicatessen's big boss and when Peter later showed up at Bob's with his lay-off papers from the huge hospital, Shear was happy to hire him. For one dollar more than he was making at the hospital, Peter started his restaurant career at the controls of the business' four big fryers. He had to peel eight bags of New Brunswick russet potatoes between six and nine in the morning, wash them, put them one by one through the manual slicer nailed to the wooden table, and blanche the resulting twenty-four buckets of potato twigs before eleven-fifteen, which was the time he gulped down a soup-of-the-day and a sandwich made with the cold cuts reserved for staff. Then Peter would change his apron, put on a little white chef's cap and take up his position in the front at the fryers. Peter also learned the words that were necessary to his survival. "Thank you, Mr. Shear. No problem. Yes, any time. Yes, I like your cheese cake."

At around five in the afternoon, after several hundred orders of fries, Peter had to filter the boiling oil from his four machines; at five-twenty, before the dinner rush, he was allowed to have a thin slice of cheese cake that hadn't been sold the day before. Peter ended his day at seven in the evening, when he handed his post over to a fellow countryman from Kastoria.

Mr. Shear was satisfied with Peter's work and, after twenty-six months of loyal service at the fryers, let him know that he'd been chosen to handle his precious slabs of smoked beef.

After his promotion to the main counter, Peter sliced smoked meat for twenty-two years at Bob's before he decided to prove to his tribe that he, too, could succeed in the restaurant business. To get enough money together, or because anything else would have been impossible, he had to team up with two newly-arrived cousins from Athens and with his brother-in-law

Stavros, in order to solidify the relationship.

Once they were in business, the two Athenians refused to wash the dishes and Stavros, who was older than Peter, naturally assumed his position at the cash register. An automatic smoked meat slicer had been purchased and, with each order, the meat could be heard squealing almost as unhappily as the non-native business associates. Poor Peter was running from one end of the business to the other, trying to save face and maintain peace. Since he was the only one with experience, he had to marinate the cabbage, skim the grease off the soups, get the turkey ready for the club sandwich, oil the slicer, supervise the wait staff, do the books, fight with the suppliers, negotiate with the bank, and humble himself before the leaseholders.

When he came into Vimont, smelling strongly of deli spice, the man appeared shrunken, like an animal that's been worn out. Peter asked to talk to me, and Martha automatically told him we weren't looking for kitchen help. Luckily, the Greek found the strength to insist. Because he wanted to talk to me about a wonderful restaurant that was for sale, not too far from our own. A well-built restaurant that was almost brand new and had an open kitchen like in my other places. Of course, the location wasn't the best, it was in a half-empty shopping center and pretty far off the street, but it was good for me to have a few reasons to argue over the price.

Peter's tragedy brought tears to my eyes, but Labelle

Boulevard, where his deli was located, was nothing but a huge used car lot. Sellers of cars and of adventures, garages, and semi-automatic car wash tunnels forced us to stay in the deli's parking lot for a few weeks, thinking things over. It took the same time for the leaseholder to soften his requirements, and to find the few thousand dollars that were required for the down payment.

Peter Papathanassopoulos had sliced smoked meat for twenty-two years without shedding a single tear, but that morning, his last on Labelle Boulevard, he was crying as he cut the thin ribbon over the only dream he ever dared try to make come true. He insisted on keeping his automatic slicer, and the brown paper distributor that he would use to wrap up his precious sandwiches in another location.

I was also crying the morning we signed the contract, both tears of joy and tears of sorrow for poor Peter.

"We'll have to renovate it pretty fast so the businesses in the shopping centre don't have to go too long without a place to eat lunch," said our clear-headed Julia.

"We'll have to split the seed again and build an independent team right away," added the practical Léna.

The real estate giant insisted that I take on the lease myself, and this requirement made me realise that I was beginning to become valuable. Another realization concerned our decision to close at three in the afternoon. Until then, we'd done it automatically as that was a normal closing time for a snack bar. But here, in the middle of a shopping centre with a *Super C* and a Jean Coutu pharmacy, there was no particular time when the customers would come and when they would leave. On the first Thursday after we opened, we realized that the middle of the afternoon is still a busy time in a shopping centre. The staff members all hesitated for a moment until Nicholas, leaving his fruit counter, grabbed the key and locked the front door. It was his first important business decision — we were a breakfast restaurant, and we closed at three. Period.

CHAPTER 59

The Expansion Continues

On Labelle Boulevard in September 1991, few children in the area thought life was actually better in school, but, inside my head, hundreds of crazy elves were sticking their tongues out at me. Peter had warned me not to close at three.

"You have to take what you can get in this insane business," he'd begged as he wrapped up his slicer.

His former boss, Mr. Shear, had often repeated: "We have to break eggs in the morning, serve our Reuben sandwich at noon, and never refuse to make a pizzaghetti in the evening.

"You don't have the luxury of having an opinion, Madame Cora," continued Peter. "Because you, too, are going to lose everything in a short time. And if you don't believe me, go look in our freezer, there's still scampi in there. The customers wanted scampi on Saturday night and when I finally started serving it, they started asking for chicken parmesan!"

***

Inspired by Peter's remarks, the leader of the dark gang decided it was time to get rid of my guardian angel for good. In my head, I witnessed the fight between the opposing forces.

"You're full of pride! Do you really think you can do better than all those who have come before you?" shouted the most repulsive elf.

"Have you thought about how high the rent is?" one of his friends then asked. "And you think you'll be able to make a profit? Tell me how such expensive rent will get paid with egg shells and short work days?"

"Did you think about where you are on the street?" added another ugly devil. "Did you think about how you can't be seen, and how there are no Quebecois living in the area? It's not enough to have a good idea; it's not enough to be nice in business."

"Sure, you've all been lucky up to now, but don't push it!" declared a sombre imp.

I felt like I was hearing my mother's voice again. As if a remote-controlled ghost was offering her favourite speech: "Cora! It's not as easy as you think. You have to earn a living by the sweat of your brow. It's written in the Scripture. Stop thinking there's enough for everybody. It's not true. We are not the lucky ones, and you know it. Stop thinking you're smarter than everyone else. God doesn't like prideful people. Listen to me for once. Stop tempting fate! Otherwise the Lord will punish you and you'll lose everything. Believe me, Cora, we're not in charge on this earth."

"But, Mother..." I replied to the accusing hordes. "I've been working seven days a week for five years, I've taken risks. I forced my children to get by with very little, and the worst thing is that I'm haunted by doubts: what more do I need to succeed? What makes you say success is not for me? I'm almost positive that God loves me, and that he wants what's best for me. I know he won't let me down. His angels are protecting me. I can see them, I can feel them. I can even hear them whispering me answers when I need them."

Organizing the fourth business had sapped my energy and delegating suddenly became easier.

"You have to trust life, trust the young people around you, and your own children," whispered an angel who defied the evil one's sneers.

***

Freshly painted and decorated with my handmade posters, the new restaurant quickly became a warm family place attracting hundreds of new hungry customers.

On Saint-Martin, Léna muttered that we were going to have to expand the liveable space in the basement and installed another plywood panel to make me a desk. With four locations, we needed a certain degree of organization, careful planning, and a real restaurant accounting system. Since each business had been incorporated separately, when the third location borrowed a case of bacon from the fourth, it had to be replaced within three days. Léna was the lookout. Not a single bucket of margarine could be given to an associated business without her knowing why.

I made the same lunch menus for the four restaurants and every head chef made a good soup and a dessert of the day, of his own choosing.

I managed the successful opening of the Labelle Boulevard restaurant without spending a single day in the kitchen. From the beginning, we'd formed a team under the leadership of a head waitress who'd been promoted to manager. I could then spend my time supervising the bigger picture; working in the basement with Léna, we would both evaluate the success of each location according to the weekly reporting forms I'd designed myself.

Without realizing it – and I wouldn't really understand for several years – I myself had established the base of a multi-branch network. We were managing our establishments from a distance and assuring that our customers would find the same quality of food and service in each of the CORA locations.

Imagine me, the most undisciplined mother in the world, the artist who couldn't write a single word without dressing it up with at least two or three different landscapes. Me, I was now insisting that a specific way of doing things be followed down to the letter. Wow!

As time went by, I designed each one of the forms we would need to run our business: time sheets, sales reports, statistics, employee evaluations, employment applications, and even a specific demand for applicants to "draw a tree."

I had read somewhere that a tree symbolized life. And when you ask someone to draw one, it shows you how they see things. We experienced hundreds of deep yet convictionless roots, the generosity of little birds chirping in branches, and the optimism of an abundance of fruit; the blue sky standing for joy, the way the tree is placed on the sheet of paper revealing cowardice or bravery; fences, snakes in the branches, a little lake on the horizon, and, sometimes, from the pencils of the most enterprising candidates, came a tractor or a platform to pile the harvest on.

***

Since I'd traded the hot griddle for the cold plywood of administration, I was concerned with another kind of competence. I gathered information about business management; about how to plan goals and where to find the information that was necessary to move forward. Evenings were spent at the coffee table in my living room, which looked increasing like a university seminar room. I copied rules down everywhere, in notebooks, on pads, and, occasionally, a key word would find its way onto the palm of my own hand. The more I studied, the easier it became to study. As disciplined as a cat tracking a mouse, I decided to do everything, learn everything and try everything so the little CORA houses would slip out of my head and come alive right before my eyes.

Several times, the demon managed to convince me that success wouldn't last; that a sheriff would show up the next day with our unpaid equipment bills; that the current success of our restaurants was temporary and that people would stop loving our food.

Satan implied that the Vimont CORA was too big, that Mrs. Labonté was better than us, that Julia would never come back from her trip to Mexico, or that our dear solicitor Chouchou was on death's door after being poisoned by a *creton* sandwich. Once he managed to grab my attention, the destructive one didn't give up. The big strawberry crêpes sagged on the plate; people hated the TEN STORY OMELETTE, and what kind of idea was it to make people eat fruit in the morning?

"Yuck! The Quebecois will never go for spinach in a crêpe!" repeated the diabolic imp.

Still, I learned to live despite all the crazy ideas the devil whispers to anyone who dares to persevere. The crêpes were delicious and other reporters mentioned our excellent breakfasts in the big daily papers. We trained several cooks in the delicate preparation of eggs, and our way of doing business was being perfected as we went along. At the Labelle Boulevard fruit counter, Nicholas started writing the first illustrated manual for the different fruit dishes that the chain's future fruiters could use. The lunch menus were being made in advance and sent to the different locations with an explanation for each dish.

***

Late in 1991, I finally had to admit that everybody loved our breakfasts and that the planet was in favour of our expansion.

In 1992, a big Cora sun appeared in the scenery of four Montreal suburbs: Rosemère, Terrebonne, Brossard, and Saint-Eustache. At the beginning of the next year, the success of our business confirmed that new restaurant concept had finally emerged from the cabbage patch in my head. The rest of my body was slowly becoming a nuclear reactor coordinating the precious propagation of our technology. It goes without saying that my fiery intention had no choice but to burst forth into a wonderful series of roles for which, once again, I had no particular aptitude.

CHAPTER 60

A CORA Franchise

ONE FINE MORNING, A VERY PRETTY YOUNG WOMAN TURNED up in the Saint-Martin basement, along with an unemployed Moroccan engineer. She wanted a "CORA" of her own!

"A CORA? We can certainly talk about it, Miss. What's your name?"

"We want a CORA just for Sophie!" declared the engineer, whose head was nearly completely shaved.

"I don't want to be your associate. I am entirely capable of setting up a restaurant. I want a franchise," the bossy girl rushed to add.

"A franchise? Young lady, I don't know what you're looking for!"

"I want a CORA franchise where I live in Pointe-Claire. I'm sure the English people who live on the West Island will love your breakfasts."

"Just a minute! What exactly is a franchise?"

"It's like a McDonald's," replied the wise engineer. "We own the restaurant, and you are the franchisor."

"The franchisor?"

"That's right, you watch me apply the system you have in place in your own restaurants!"

"Hmmm... I really have to think all this over, and get some information about franchising. I'll let you know when I'm ready to talk again."

I devoured all the franchising books in the business school library before I even thought again about Mademoiselle Sophie's request. And, to my great surprise, I discovered the young lady was right: I was an ideal candidate to become a franchisor. The CORA concept met almost every criteria listed by the most famous franchise lawyer in Québec.

CHEZ CORA was a new idea, different from everything else that already existed in the food industry, advocating a better way of doing things and offering its customers a wide array of new products. One of its best, nearly universal features was answering a fundamental need shared by all people, of all walks of life, from all over the world — the need to eat. The "concept" also offered many possibilities for growth, both for a future enterprising franchisor like me, and for a franchisee who could acquire several locations. The way we worked was relatively simple and easy to teach. Hadn't we already illustrated this when we'd trained our independent teams?

The only legal restrictions a location would have to

comply with would be those concerning hygiene and health measures for the food industry. Since there were already eight restaurants, it would be easy to show profitability and, more importantly, it would now be possible to define and measure the causes of its success. A CHEZ CORA restaurant was very attractive for a future franchisee because of the quality of its products, the proven business techniques, and the recipes that so many customers had already given their stamp of approval to. As well, the reduced work hours were very tempting because they offered a better quality of life, for the employees and our partners, the franchisees.

Finally, the CORA project was financially very realistic, given the simplicity of the décor, the reasonable amount of equipment required, and its relatively modest furnishings.

Once again, the big YES was fighting to rise into my mouth when the young West Island woman called to me from the other end of a phone line.

"Yes, Sophie, I remember you. Yes! You can stop by, but come on a weekday, after three o'clock."

***

When the young woman came down the Saint-Martin stairs this time, she was preceded by the perfectly pressed trouser leg of a fifty-year-old man whose salt-and-pepper hair contrasted surprisingly with the child-like light in his eyes.

"Cora, I've been waiting for your call for three weeks. I've brought my uncle along so he could explain franchising to you."

"Hello, I... I've done some research and it looks more complicated than I thought to become a franchisor. You need contracts, recipe books, procedure books, forms, and very specific rules that you must then make sure are enforced."

"Oh, don't let all that paperwork bog you down! Franchising isn't as difficult as you think! Especially when you start with a great idea like yours."

"Sir, it's not the franchising that's complicated. It's doing it right. I did some research and I think the idea of franchising is marvellous for a lady like me whose dream is to see her restaurants all across North America. But writing the franchise contract is something else again! And the business manual is even worse, according to my daughter."

"Stop worrying! Rome wasn't built in a day! You'll cross that bridge when you come to it. When I started, I opened a cleaning service. My nearest competitor thought I'd come up with a helluva good way of hanging the pressed clothes on a moving rack connected to a button by the till. When the cashier pressed the button, Mr. X's suit came right to her, which was a great savings in time because she didn't have to go all the way to the back room to get it. My competitor asked me to install the same set-up in his place, in exchange for a bit of cash, of course! Believe it or not, that night

I wrote my first franchise contract on the back of the placemat in the little restaurant where we'd gone to have a coffee. Today, and especially since our merger with DaJuin, I can't even keep up with our chain's progress. You and Sophie just have to agree on the main rules of the game, the rest will come with time. You have to keep developing because what you've got on your hands is an excellent business opportunity."

"Thank you, sir. You've got quite a talent there for simplifying life."

"Don't worry, life is just a big play and I get up on stage almost every day.[5] Keep working on your project; it's super, and it's time for the rest of us to be able to eat your amazing food. In business, like in anything else, you have to put one foot in front of the other if you want to make any progress; there's no use pretending you're going to iron the American flag if you can't even iron your neighbour's trousers properly! You look like you're full of vim and vigour; you're a strong, God-fearing woman, you know your crêpes, you have everything you need to succeed. It's no more complicated than that. Business isn't just for some special kind of phoenix. Business is for ordinary people, like you and me, because people like us aren't afraid to get their hands dirty or to go knock on the door of a new client. And besides, think about it, if you go into franchising, you're going to help a bunch of people get into business without too much risk, and show them how to do it and avoid the worst. My mother used to say, 'Mikey, if you

[5] Sophie's uncle is also a famous actor in Québec.

help save a soul, you save your own.' Well, Cora, I'm here to tell you that if you help someone else to succeed in business, you'll succeed yourself!"

***

Nonetheless, our preparations took an entire year as I read every franchise contract I could get my hands on, along with a few examples of franchising manuals that some companies made public. My children and I also spent months fighting over the amounts of different ingredients for the recipes because, up until then, we'd been eyeballing, with four apples, eight soup bowls from the first snack bar, or enough starch to thicken the mixture. We had to meticulously reproduce, in front of witnesses, each of the recipes, as we precisely measured the quantities, the cooking times, and the exact amount that each set of instructions should produce. We had to dissect the beautiful bird of my dreams, seek the root of each gesture, explain why and how, and quantify the when. And, I went back to my pencil and notebooks, but not to write the CHEZ CORA novel. Instead, I wrote down the practical details of how everything worked. And, according to the experts, we did it better than any other beginners in this profession.

We weren't really just getting started, since, without really realizing it, I'd already discovered and had been using the rules for a network of multiple locations. We had a great deal of experience in preparing breakfasts and our customer service had been described as excellent. What I still had to do was organise more systematic supervision of the different restaurants and master the art of offering good advice as a franchising partner, rather than giving orders as a big boss.

In order to simplify the organisational structure of the new franchising entity, I offered my associates in certain existing restaurants the opportunity to buy my shares and become franchisees or, if they didn't agree, they could sell their shares to me and then I would sell the restaurant to a new franchisee.

In the spring of 1994, after everything was polished up, we set Sophie up with a big CORA sun hanging over the Terrarium shopping centre, at the intersection of Hymus Boulevard and Saint-Jean Boulevard in Pointe-Claire. The new CORA opened and it was as wonderful as the ones the founder had given birth to herself. It was an obvious success for CHEZ CORA, to be so perfectly reproduced, in accordance with a contract, and, of course, in exchange for a few dollars.

We were jubilant and coordinated the opening of seven other franchises, which, in the following year, would thrust us into the position of "the breakfast leader of Quebec."

In July 1995, Julia left the family business to spread her own wings elsewhere. Titan continued to reach for the sky by stacking one mountain on top of the other, and Nicholas slipped expertly from the fruit station to the griddle. My youngest son decided to commit to the CORA kitchen because, at the time, nothing interested him more. Slowly, his circle of interest went beyond the sound of the pots and pans; and, replacing Julia, he became responsible for opening the chain's next twenty restaurants.

***

In the spring of 1996, the new franchisor team hit an uncomfortable plateau. Too young to behave like a seasoned business, it was coming to terms with a network that was already too impressive to settle for strictly home-made leadership. It became urgent for our core to learn from outside experts. I had to admit that we had, for the time being at least, reached the summit of our abilities. We needed to leave our comfort zone and look towards other brains that were filled with concrete knowledge about franchising. I looked for them and I found them. Then, after that, thanks to the perfectly-timed arrival of a network management specialist whose task was to simplify what we were doing and solidify our potential, the management team improved even more and managed to grow at an even faster rate. I started to learn to delegate, along with the technique of side-stepping. I would realize much later that being able to hire people who were better-qualified than me is the act of a real CEO.

The new manager called himself the executive vice-president and was quick to award titles to all those around him. Nicholas was given the title "Director of Operations" and I got the prestigious "Founding President," in case I could forget who I was!

I was proud of the progress made by that little seed that Providence had once planted in my head. I was savouring the experience of having given birth to such a phenomenon. Being in business was as painful, and as exciting as motherhood. It's a kind of unending public labour, that involves absolutely all of us and uses all our strength, and requires the same determination a mother shows when she wants to be sure her child arrives in this world safe and sound.

The more the business grew, the more I felt out of my depth. Luckily, I was surrounded by experienced coworkers, and I was happy to delegate things to them. I understood I didn't have to know how to do everything, especially since I'd read Henry Ford's biography to encourage myself. At the end of the day, the prestigious title said it all: my role was to preside over the business, to embody it, to represent it, to describe it to others, to make sure it had all the resources it needed, and to enrich it as often as possible with my ideas. I didn't get my hands on the spatula much anymore, but like a good conductor, I was leading the orchestra. I'd tap my magic wand here and there, and save the last bow for myself.

It was relatively easy to accept responsibility for the

final decision because I'd always had a big, enterprising YES, ready to jump out of my mouth. I'm the one whose heart had always carried CHEZ CORA'S precious yeast. Yes, we'll sell our house to buy *Miss Côte-Vertu*; yes, we'll serve real crêpes; yes, we'll buy Saint-Martin; yes to the pork roast; yes to Vimont; yes to Peter's restaurant; yes to franchising; yes to the vice-president; and yes, I learned to calm down when my inner voice fell silent. I had to trust my intuition and wait for it to give me a sign. That little voice was like a computer smart chip between my ears — its perfect externalization was the state of grace I found myself in.

Deciding always carries the risk of being wrong, and it requires as much courage as it does humility. If choices were always obvious, there'd be no decisions to make, we'd just have to notice we had to turn a little more to the left or push a little more to the right. You have to have the courage to come to a decision in due course, and the humility to beg for the information you need to evaluate the consequences of your choices. I never rushed to make a decision. Most of the time I insisted on sleeping on it, as they say. The truth is, I was waiting for something obvious to awaken in me; I was waiting for my main strategist (my guardian angel) to send me the essential information. When nothing would come, I'd go for a drive, watch movies, talk about the project with my coworkers, listen, draw, ask for more explanations, size things up, put data together, and become a sort of catalyst for the information. When a decision appeared and took shape, I'd answer YES. Otherwise, I'd step back. Sometimes, I'd look like a complete fool, and I know a lot of people have questioned my competence; that doesn't really matter to me. The important thing was to win. The main thing was to move forward in harmony, with my heart facing the same direction as my nose.

In business, there are risks; but when you start with nothing, you have nothing to lose and you can allow yourself to take a few risks. Then, if you take enough of them, you learn to measure their reach. It's unavoidable. I'm very careful; I don't waste money that I haven't earned yet. I learned that from Granddad Frédéric who always used to say you shouldn't count your chickens before they're hatched, and you should never bite off more than you can chew. I couldn't needlessly borrow even if, sometimes, it was detrimental to the banks that would have liked to work with me; even if nowadays they write books to teach courageous people how to make money with other people's money.

***

My entrepreneurial story is really quite simple in the end. I drew myself, as Walt Disney said, with what I had at hand. Just like back when I was living with Aunt Olivette, I'd build myself up again every time the wind insisted on blowing down my house of cards. When I opened the first *Chez Cora*, I just wanted to survive my burnout, move on, and feed my children. I listened to my heart and decided to make people happy. I acted, not out of interest or controlled by any real strategy, but because I personally needed so much love and personal satisfaction.

"Come on, sir! Have another bowl of chowder, it won't cost you any more. Come on, it's your favourite soup."

"Give Betty a double portion of custard. The poor thing's got a twelve-hour shift to do at Pharmaprix."

"Yes, Bastien, I made you some real *cretons*, with a recipe I got from a priest's housekeeper. And have a piece of fudge made with thirty five per cent cream."

I spent hundreds of afternoons trying out recipes for caramel sauce, green ketchup, and waffle mix before any of them were added to our menu. I made mocha bars for Jean-Claude, gingerbread Christmas trees for Nico, macaroons, and all sorts of little things with fresh seasonal fruit. I liked to create lunch specials; inventing crazy names for the sandwiches, the stuffed burgers, and the Italo-Greco-Quebecois pastas. I always placed a lot of importance on little details that might make people happy. And I wasn't shy about bugging everyone with my poetic meal descriptions. One day, just to tease the Greek half of my young Nicholas, I invented the story of THE GREEK COUNTRY SALAD and sent it to all the cooks in the network.

CHAPTER 61

The Greek Country Salad

It's called a Greek Country Salad because when the Greek grandma notices it's almost time to eat, she takes off her slippers, puts on her old wooden clogs, and walks out to the garden at the back of the family yard. She plucks seven or eight big tomatoes from the vine and picks up two happy cucumbers lying in the furrow she's walking in and then grabs a nice red pepper that the crows have spared.

Then, she pulls the tails of a few shallots and looks for a sprig of oregano. Hobbling along, she hides her lunch in her apron, climbs over the bramble fence, crosses the field of Karayiannopoulos cottonwood trees, and goes to Maria's olive shop because she's the only one who'll agree to trade her a few black pearls for her extra tomatoes.

Add a thick slice of feta cheese to the nicely chopped vegetables.

Sprinkle with olive oil and red wine vinegar.

Top with fresh chopped oregano.

P.S. Always cover the delicious salad with a grilled pita.

Because the Greek grandma also picks up one or two pita on her way to say hello to Michali, her grandson who, although he's only fifteen, is already working for Papou Costa, the best baker in all Peloponnesia.

CHAPTER 62

Pumpkin Cream Soup

SOMETIMES, JUST FOR FUN, I SEND AN EDITORIAL TO THE franchisees with a lesson hidden in the cookie.

> *Hello, dear cooks! Halloween is on its way.*
>
> *What scares me more than ten rabid black cats fighting over the doormat in front of my place, more than an incredibly ugly old 118-year-old witch in the backseat of my car, and more than a ghost asking to borrow a dime to make a phone call, I admit it, what scares me most, as I strut proudly around a* CORA *restaurant, is coming across an undercooked, flabby spinach and cheddar omelette sitting on a big oval plate with its belly glistening with oil and its edges*

uneven. It's worse than seeing a warty toad who's decided to climb up a big strawberry shortcake.

I'm not exaggerating when I say how much I'm afraid of seeing a bad CORA *breakfast; either overcooked or undercooked, too fat or too thin, flat or underripe, with its yolk broken, tasteless and unworthy of the customer's high expectations. I'm afraid of this because our customers come to us because they want to eat, to give themselves a treat, to have something tasty, and to be delighted. I'm afraid of this because in our restaurants, food is the most important thing; not beer, not peanuts in their shells, or their neighbour's see-through top. We're popular because of our food, and our food is what all our customers talk about. I guarantee you that the day our dishes start looking like Halloween costumes... well, that day (and I pray it never comes), that day, my dear friends, we can forget our paying jobs, our profitable investments, tennis at three-forty-five, our country décor, or the new ultrafast rotary toaster. Because the day when we're not the best anymore, we'll already be part of the worst. And those are the ones who have to settle for paper handkerchiefs when they cry. Ooh!*

Because my note had given him a good laugh, Dominic, the Vimont cook, sent me his favourite pumpkin soup recipe.

Dice and place the following in a pot:

6 cups of pumpkin
4 cups of carrots
4 cups of potatoes
1 cup of onion

Cook all the above ingredients in water, drain, and put them through the food processor. Then place the puréed mixture back in the pot and add two cups of water, three cups of milk, a half teaspoon of ginger, and a few teaspoons of butter.

Heat and stir until it comes to a simmer. When serving, add a few croutons cut into the shape of a bat to each customer's bowl.

Thanks, Dominic!

CHAPTER 63

Conquer Your Own Beliefs

When I was little, my father used to say, "The big jobs are in Toronto. Learn English and typing and settle for being a good bilingual secretary."

Deep in our Gaspésie, we'd had to settle for crumbs and we were supposed to feel lucky that we could eat three times a day. In the village, the people who'd succeeded didn't have "much of a conscience" or were capable of "playing with other people's money in order to get rich." I remember how our neighbours used to gossip in our kitchen; one day, they were talking about Mr. Leblanc, the debauched owner of the village's first movie theatre; another, they talked about Napoléon Babin, the boot-licker, who, according to what people said, got all his digging permits directly from Father Rioux's hands. The only thing they didn't say outright was that rich people were all thieves. When you grow up with this kind of mentality, it's practically impossible to become a business leader. It's forbidden, it may even be a sin, to think about getting rich. And it's even worse, I suppose, if you're a woman who's decided not to settle for a supporting role and who's decided to take control of her own existence. You feel marginalized, selfish, and under constant threat of the punishment reserved for those who disobey the rules.

Luckily, I never learned to love money. I was therefore never motivated by it when I started working. I just wanted to feed my children and become somebody.

I really wanted to become someone good, someone who'd done enough to deserve to be loved. My whole life I tried to figure out the mystery around the existence of God and I prayed that the Supreme Being would give me some of his attention.

I never really understood why I was so sure I had a future waiting for me, and I also don't know where I found the willpower to devote myself to it. I also don't know where I found the knowledge to make the right decisions to grow my business. But one thing I did know deep in my heart was that love was the most important thing. I loved my children, my imaginary creations, my poetry, and my new breakfast concept like they were the most important things on earth.

We weren't taught to express our emotions, whether we felt happiness or fear, and we certainly never learned it was necessary to express ourselves. As for the rest of our education, our parents handed it off to the school and the school assumed we'd gotten it at home. This is why my brother, my sisters, and I came into the world with the most important parts of us amputated, feeling incapable, and convinced we were inferior.

What better place than a field of manure to dream of roses? What better example than an empty restaurant to understand what success is? What better than darkness to learn the benefits of light, and a dry desert to mentally remember water's extraordinary taste?

I bit into an awful lot of those nuggets of misery before I understood: they'd been specially prepared to help me appreciate a bigger feast. I understood that all of this world's reality is just theatre; it's a big play, like the famous actor had said — a play where each of us plays a role, our own role. Above all, I understood that this whole planet is the context where we experiment with what it means to be human. I also understood that I wasn't really of this world, since none of the actors are nailed to the boards where they give their performances. I finally understood that what I call the soul, or the heart, or usually the mind, is God living inside of me. I realized He'd always been there and I'd never been separated from Him since my true nature is a part of Him. Whatever exists by day and by night, whatever thinks, whatever talks inside of me, whatever has the ability to transport me into a thousand conversations at once, whatever insists, whatever is omnipresent, is all the real me, my true nature inspiring me and telling me what abyss to avoid or what crazy idea to embrace. It was extraordinary to be suddenly freed from the fifty thousand skyscrapers that had blocked my ability to recognize this accessible paradise. Yes, love was my only true home, the place I'll return to when the curtain comes down on my own personal play. God is all there is and part of His strength is what's been fluttering in my head for as long as I've been conscious. This strength has never disappeared, and always called me towards the most sublime part of myself. I've always been attracted by the idea of outdoing myself, and today I understand that as I've been evolving, it has always been Him, the Great Manitou, taking up more and more space within me.

***

Oddly enough, it was the money linked to success that scared me the most when I was starting out. What could I do to have money and not lose my soul? I still had a lot of distance to cover on the road to financial illumination. But it was comforting to realize that the more you evolve, the more you can remember that you are a child of God, and the more money, on its own, becomes a good thing. I understood it wasn't enough just to work hard to earn the money; you also had to understand the cosmic laws of success, the virtues that attract abundance. You have to adopt a winning state of mind and firmly believe that you are the producer of your own life, the one who designs the dream, who writes the script, plays the main role on stage, and has the ultimate privilege of enjoying the applause.

If you want to succeed, you have to conquer your fears. You have to win out over your own beliefs and believe that some kind of success is available to you. It doesn't happen in the blink of an eye. And it won't happen either if you lock yourself up in a Tibetan monastery to pray. If you want to learn to believe in success, you must be calm, humble, have your two feet firmly on the ground, and your hands doing every bit of work within reach. Believing in success is like believing in heaven; it's a mental conclusion, an illumination you can come to at any moment in your life, when you're in up to your neck trying to get something to work. Believing in success means believing a glass is half full when it's half empty. This is a rare thing because fifty per cent of people will say the glass is half empty. The glass will eventually become empty all by itself, through nothing more than the natural process of evaporation. Believing in success doesn't happen because your fingers are running over the keys of your calculator or because you're starting your MBA degree. Education is like skates attached to the bottom of our boots. Often, it allows us to fly instead of crawling forward on our knees, but it doesn't guarantee we'll make it to the fiftieth floor of a high-priced office building to sign the hefty contracts.

I write so much about fear because, when I was

starting my business, my worst enemy was this terrible feeling of fear. It was stubborn and felt as if it had been made just for me. It could stand attacks of happiness, kick up a storm despite economic growth, and wasn't impressed by the most intelligent motivational speaker I could listen to.

Our head is often what turns out to be the most damaging tool as far as success is concerned. In adversity, the analytic part of us can paralyze us when things don't unfold exactly as we expect. The truth is, the events of our lives never unfold as we plan them. And this upsets us; it upsets our ego because we were wrong, and we feel like we're losing control. In my opinion, this is when negativity has the most influence on our thinking machines.

Unfortunately, there's only one thing that can be done to thwart negativity: deciding that's not how things are going to be. Change the way you look at things, see the glass as half full, roll up your sleeves and do everything you can to fill it up; try even harder, throw yourself in heart and soul, and never believe it could happen any other way. I hear so many people casually say they're going to try this or that, they're going to invest several thousand dollars here or there, they're going to wait a year or two to see if things work out. Every time, the same reply comes into my mind:

"Don't waste your time, my friend, it'll never work. Business is not a roll of the dice; it's not luck either. Business is a matter of commitment, a question of life and death for someone who's just starting out. Business is a state of mind and a vocation. When you climb on this kind of ship, you can never think that you'd be better off somewhere else. You have to give yourself over to it, body and soul, and you have to absolutely love what you do."

Our success depends on our daily decision to succeed. You have to work hard; carefully place the hotdog in the bun, so your customer has room to put on his favourite topping; have raw onions available when that's what the customer wants and Dijon mustard because that's what the customer asked for. Your chairs have to be properly stuffed, so your customers are comfortable when they sit down; carefully replace the sole if you're a shoemaker, give your brushes a good clean between clients if you're a hairstylist, be a good writer if that's how you make your living. You have to do everything right, even the tiniest details, even if no one is watching, even if you don't understand how it can possibly make any difference.

You have to do things right and listen to your customers. There's no secret about CORA's famous menu: our customers are the ones who came up with it. This menu, which has already won many prizes and for which I get regular compliments, is the result of multiple requests from customers, and the expression of every occasion I had to personally make someone happy by saying, "Sure, that's possible! I can make that for you, just let me practice a little."

It's important to know that I did not invent any new food. I just discovered new ways of doing things or of mixing two things together to make a third. And when the people around me go gaga as the dish takes shape, that's better than any other possible market study.

If you want to succeed, you have to listen to your customers, and always predict what their hearts are asking for. Frankly, the only good idea I had was to do just that. It's been my great pleasure to cook and make customers happy.

If you want to succeed, you also have to avoid asking yourself too many questions; you have to get around existential puzzles, avoid doubt, and banish eternal analysis. With a miserable childhood, an unsuccessful marriage, no knowledge of the profession, and almost nonexistent financial means, not to mention the famous "success-is-for-other-people" complex, I had, from the beginning, everything I needed to fail or to succeed. I didn't understand this until much later and at the price of enormous daily effort. It's easy to say success can be summed up as a mental decision.

"An illumination," add the nasty elves, as they laugh at what I've written.

It's something you can read in every self-help book there is; such an idea has even become a cliché. And still, it's incredibly complicated to really understand it.

Thousands of times I've said to myself — "I can't do it," "What's wrong with me?" "I'll never make it, "It's not for people like me," "I don't know enough about it," "I never should have gotten mixed up in this." And the worst part is, most of the time I didn't tell anyone about things like that. I was afraid of disappointing my children, my employees, and those that were close to me. I was ashamed of showing them I was weak, and I was ashamed of being afraid! I was panicking even though I looked like I was smiling. I imagined I was the only one who was afraid, because, all around me, everyone seemed to be doing okay. I didn't yet know that all entrepreneurs are in the same situation as me. And the ones who keep on trying despite it all are often the ones who have no choice, like immigrants who cannot return to their homeland.

Lots of times, duty forces us to conquer our fears. That's how it was for me: I had children to feed, rent and a car loan to pay, with no alimony or well-meaning relatives to depend on. "Necessity is the mother of invention," because it forces us to go beyond what we think we can do. We should see it as a blessing, but when you're starting out in business, it looks more like a curse.

It's so hard to start a business. The hours are long, there's not enough money, it's economically impossible to hire enough help, you have to fight feeling discouraged, resist gossip, isolation, and a lack of encouragement from those around you. It seems like no one is interested in your efforts or that your projects bother them. It often seems like they're just there to keep an eye on you, to wait for you to go bankrupt, as if your failure would justify their own lack of action.

Despite it all, I made progress. I was persistent, I kept slaving away, I kept my nose to the grindstone, I cried and I kept on cooking, and, to my great surprise, I discovered how much I liked it. I discovered that the creative process can be fed by any resource. I dreamed of writing, of composing novels, and here I was doing it with flour, slices of banana, spiced breads, and pieces of exotic fruit. God, you have to *love* your work. It's important to feel inspired by it, to be enthusiastic, because love of work is what helps you persevere. And persevering is a constant desire to always want to know more. Perseverance is what allowed me to move forward. Perseverance has never allowed me to give up. It's what kept me at the snack bar after closing time, looking for more ways to delight my customers. It's what fed my eternal curiosity and made me go from one stall at the market to the next. I even owe the illustrious title on my business cards to perseverance. In the course of our lives, we all have thousands of wonderful ideas, but how many of us really possess the perseverance that's necessary to work on one idea until it turns into a success? Perseverance is a kind of yeast that a helpful hand places in the heart of an entrepreneur to help him rise!

***

The reward you get from work is not the money, but

what it allows you to become. And I'm a perfect example; because I persisted, because I worked so hard with my own hands, that they became masters of what they did and their expertise gave me a great deal of confidence, and even courage. Enough courage to award myself the title "Breakfast Queen," thereby creating an excellent brand; a brand whose authenticity no one can ever question.

It was also because I liked to cook that I kept opening restaurants. I did it several times until I realized I was capable of teaching others to do so. And that's how I discovered franchising: teaching others your own recipe. That's how I became a franchising entrepreneur who dreamed of filling up all of North America with CORA restaurants. At the beginning of the new millennium, my vision was beginning to become reality. I was travelling all over the province and seeing CORAS everywhere. It made me so happy and, at the same time, it made wish to open restaurants in other places: behind big mountains, beyond enormous prairies, on the other side of wide rivers, in Ontario, in British Columbia, in the rest of Canada, and even down south! For such an odyssey to succeed, all the CORA franchisees had to have the same dream in their heads that I did. I wished they would all understand that our business was more than simply selling two crêpes for eight dollars. I dreamed they'd realized we weren't only in the food business, but in the business of making people happy and showing them love. Because what we were offering was happiness: joyful moments and delicious, unforgettable memories. I dreamed the Cora franchisees would be beacons of contentment, treat-filled islands in the fog, with fresh flowers around their necks, bright stars in their eyes, and the aroma of exotic fruit carrying their every word. I dreamed that every Cora franchisee would commit to the success of his business and that, all together, they'd make up an enormous collective brain that concentrated on our customers' delight.

***

When we opened the *Chez Cora* on Saint-Martin, I hung the picture of my late father on the little wall along the counter, and I made sure he could keep an eye on the cash register. I wanted him to see the money coming in. Then, I put up a copy of the same photo in Vimont, in Labelle, and in all of my own restaurants. Now, you can find it in the administrative office where they keep me prisoner. I hope that, from his place in heaven, my father can finally allow himself to feel proud of me.

Maybe there was no need for me to pin the photo up by the cash register, but, I thought to myself, maybe all the saints in heaven are like Saint Thomas, who had to place his finger in the Lord's wound. As for me, was a whole province's gratitude not enough to satisfy me? Undoubtedly, my heart needed a father to tell me, "Great job, Cora! You're really doing great."

CHAPTER 64

Madam President

THOUGH I'D NEVER ENVIED THE POPULARITY OF SOMEONE like Coco Chanel or Lise Watier, now, with thirty restaurants, I was in pain because I was afraid I might not be able to satisfy the needs of my own creation. Like attacking parasites, thousands of questions gnawed at my brain. Would I be a good franchisor? Was I a good enough person? Would I be able to grow? Did I know enough? It was urgent for me to put an end to such torture. And, this time, I enlisted the help of a professional business coach.

After a few weeks of introspection, I first became certain of one thing: anything the mind can conceive of or desire, it can achieve. We have everything we need to bring the ideas God sends us to maturity. Yes, all the tools are within me, or within my reach, and all I have to do is recognize them and get them for myself. The second certainty that occurred to me was that the business was my own. I was the one who'd created it, and it was up to me to manage it, rather than to be its victim; it was my theatre, my script, and there was nothing for me to be afraid of. I was allowed to make mistakes, like every human being, but no one could push me out of my own creation, unless I permitted it. I could take my time and I had the privilege of being able to repair my blunders; besides, my errors were nothing but detours on the road to success, or maybe they were shortcuts or alternative solutions that it wasn't to my advantage to choose. Oof! What a relief it was to understand all that. As I learned to contemplate my accomplishments, I learned to accept my ability to succeed; I made the decision myself, and I decided to go as far as possible. I just had to speak clearly with the people I would be working with and they'd follow me because I was the source and the vital energy behind the first concept. I loved my business and I'd decided to devote my life to it. I'd never dream of doing anything but serving. I'd never hesitate again. I was the Cora on the sign, I was the first one who'd said:

"Of course, Mr. Smith. We can bring you brown toast."

"Why not, Mrs. Thomson? We can replace the peanut butter with chocolate spread on your grandson's dish."

"Certainly we can give you two slices of tomato instead of the home-fried potatoes."

"No, we won't ask you to pay for your second cup

of coffee, or even the third, but please let me know if you don't have enough cream."

I learned to count my blessings, to recognize my talents and to appreciate my accomplishments. Seeing what I'd made come true helped me have confidence in myself; if I'd managed to open eight restaurants and keep them running, I could do the same with eighteen, fifty-eight, 208, and even more, with no problem. I knew how to organize things and do whatever was necessary to keep things moving.

With the help of my children, I took the time to define our business's mission. Together, we set the standards for the behaviour and values that would govern our future actions.

I reaffirmed my intention to leave my mark on this world; to leave something better behind; something to be remembered besides a name on a poster. I wanted to contribute, in my own way, to other people's well-being. Above all, I wanted my concept to keep evolving through me. I learned to control my thinking, to be in charge of it, rather than being subjected to its ups-and-downs.

With my mind reenergized, I committed to being a franchisor, and to being one of the most competent, upright, and progressive of all. Each of my commitments was based on a principle from our business's new mission statement: "Becoming the international leader in breakfast specialties, by offering our guests top quality food and service in a warm, family atmosphere." I also committed to the fact that future entrepreneurs should be able to reach their maximum potential by using our business model. Today, I firmly believe that it's my personal deep commitment to allow each one of my dreams to become a reality that launched my business into the future.

Different and better, from one day to the next, CHEZ CORA became my manuscript, the creative text of my own life: the good times, the problems, and all the ludicrous circumstances that revealed to me who I really was.

***

Neither my childhood in Gaspésie nor my education prepared me to become a chief executive officer. However both worked together to solidify my resistance to adversity and helped me develop a kind of survival instinct that forced me to get organized early on. Other people's indifference towards me sharpened my will and spurred me, many times, to go beyond what others did. In this way, my personality learned to set itself apart in such a way that my leading roles seemed to fall from the sky. Even though I was stuck between an oven and a filing cabinet, I wanted to learn all I could. I took the bull by the horns and went deeper into everything until my research became a passion. By doing this, the vibrant love I developed for DÉJEUNER CORA became the binder my destiny needed to become reality. It just took a long time for me to understand that it had all been useful.

***

Life is so wonderfully conceived it makes me want to cry. Things arrive at exactly the right time, in a head or heart that is ready to receive them. Until we have the opportunity to learn this, we suffer. We bluster about because we can't understand what's happening to us. Since we can't yet see our whole life laid out in a photograph, we can't accept that A and B come before C, that E paves the way for F, that G is necessary for H, and that N always comes after M. Today we're drying out because we've forgotten that there will be rain tomorrow. Sometimes we act as if the sun was about to set for the last time.

The paradox of success is that you have to keep making progress, move forward, always keep active and, at the same time, you must let go, know how to wait, trust, be still, and listen. You have to be ambitious and detached at the same time; you have to be ready to go all the way and ready to step back. You have to be voracious and frugal, passionate and thoughtful, strict and warm, humble and proud. You have to be able to stir up a crowd and to tolerate being alone. And first work on yourself, so you can work better with others.

When you're a boss, you're alone with responsibility, alone with worry and with the final decision. Isolation, like taking risks, eventually becomes a habit. It hardens us, it builds our character. Personally, I think of that solitude as a kind of electricity that I alone possess; it's the silence where I receive my divine replies.

***

I became convinced that I could succeed at anything I put my mind to, because I understood that success is a matter of time: the time it takes to practice what you excel at, the time it takes to start over again and again until you can do one thing perfectly. Think of Lindbergh, who tried to cross the Atlantic forty-eight times before he succeeded. I know most pilots would have gotten off the plane after the third or fifth attempt, once every possible excuse had passed before their eyes.

I'm successful because I never give up. I turn, I change, I negotiate until the thing looks the way I want it to look. In my head, I never stop making plans. Like when I used to play with Aunt Olivette's cards. I'd try to improve my palace by adding a little wall. I'd look for ideas, I'd read, I'd pray, I'd listen to tapes, I'd keep two or three conversations going on at once, then I'd settle down so the wind wouldn't carry away what I'd built.

"Fake it till you make it," Titan used to tell me when it came to buying an old used Mercedes. "Successful people drive Mercedes. Why shouldn't you, Mom?"

And he was right; every morning, the wonderful hood ornament would invite me to climb into the car and fly off towards my destiny. As far as anything else was concerned, I didn't know a thing about cars, or any of the accessories my old German carriage was unfortunately lacking. What was important is how I felt when I heard the aristocratic purr of the diesel engine. Handsome Marcel from Côte-Vertu would have laughed at such feminine considerations. He would have pointed out that the noise I loved so much sounded like the one the old Hussman compressor used to make when summer took a run at its innards.

I always considered myself much more a mother, or even a mother hen, than a business woman. Therefore I never felt that my gender deprived me of any possibilities. My best cards are still my endurance, my tenacity, the way I can make a good dinner out of next to nothing, and the compassion I can show a crane operator at the end of a ten-hour shift. It doesn't really matter what gender you are when you have to get your head above water. You hesitate, you flounder, you swallow some water, you swim, you push on and eventually you get to the shore, whether you're a man or a woman or a baboon. Success is about attitude, not biceps. Of course, you have to have some of the smaller muscles, the kind that are given out to both sexes, and you have to be able to use those head muscles if you want to climb the steps up to the bank. You have to make up for the hundreds of years head start men have in coming up with business plans, while we females were cooking or washing the babies' diapers. But you can't feel needy or penalized when you go to a financial institution. If we didn't want more, men probably never would have had the idea of saving three cents in order to impress us.

Like my Greek ex-husband used to say: women are lacking in a lot of things. Among these things are the fact that *we* always underestimate ourselves by thinking *we're* missing something, by thinking *we're* inferior. We are neither better nor worse than men, we're just different.

Women are so much greater than the roles they often give themselves. They are, in my opinion, much better prepared to succeed in business. Especially mothers, because they are the ones who suffer to expel life; they feed, protect, snuggle, wait, scold, educate, watch over and then, in the end, they cope with the difficulty of the teenage years. They save money for bread, figure out the number of bottles their babies will need each night, measure the hours between each spoonful of medicine, and write down the precious date of the first tooth or the last poop in a diaper. Women are less self-assured, a psychologist would say, and, in my opinion, it's better because it makes them have to rely more on their intuition, which is never wrong. Because they don't take success for granted, women are more meticulous, more careful and less impulsive. Women examine a situation from every angle before they make a decision.

***

Thank God I never had to fight to show my worth, because I started out at the right place. I started at the stove and, when the time came to take off my apron, it was already too late to get caught up worrying about things like "I'm not as competent as my neighbour Paul." As a woman, I am lucky enough to be healthy as a horse, as full of energy as a marathon runner. I can concentrate remarkably well for an old 1947 model, and I am a leader. I can inspire discipline in all the people I work with as well as all the necessary enthusiasm to fulfill our mission. After my guardian angel, I am the business's principal strategist, and I have learned that I am very good at enlarging the scope of our expertise as we grow. It's my responsibility as leader to communicate that strategy, to keep it up to date, and be certain it's engraved in the hearts of all my colleagues.

I like freedom, the freedom to think, to spend, to say and to do what I want. This kind of freedom is like an airplane motor drawing wide circles around my ideas and equipping them with turboprops.

Because I dreamed of seeing a face sparkle with happiness, a fiery kind of energy made me go beyond the limits of what was known and gave me a taste for the unusual. Since the opening of the first *Chez Cora*, no other music has caught my attention as much as the sizzling of *crespelles* on the griddle, no other work of art has been more original that the MAGIC breakfast, and no single day has been more interesting than the one I spent searching the supermarket for new ways of delighting my customers.

CHAPTER 65

GARGANTUA

"GRANDMA, TELL ME WHAT YOU USED TO LEARN IN SCHOOL when you were little," baby Alex asked me when he was eleven.

"Eat your sausages, little one. Grandma used to learn Latin and the history of the old days."

"Grandma, why did you name what I'm eating the GARGANTUAN breakfast?"

"My little monkey! It's because Gargantua was a giant who ate a lot, just like you."

"Why was the giant called Gargantua?" my grandson asked.

"Because a long time ago, in the country where Granddad Jaco and King Charlemagne used to live, there was an incredible giant who could eat more all by himself than all the people in his whole town put together. The giant was the son of a princess called Gargamelle and wealthy merchant called Grandgousier.

They named the baby Gargantua because of what happened when he was born. When he came out of his mommy's tummy, instead of crying like you did, that baby started shouting, 'I want something to drink! I want something to drink!' His father stepped over to his crib and exclaimed, '*Que grand tu as! Que grand tu as!*' That means, 'How big you are! How big you are!' And everyone who was there thought that it sounded like 'gar-gan-tua,' and they decided that must be the baby's name, since those were the first words the father spoke when he saw his son. Grandgousier and the mother Gargamelle agreed with this name. They say it took thirteen thousand cows to feed baby Gargantua, and when he was one and a half, he already had eighteen chins, and if you wanted to get his attention, you just had to let him see a couple of plates of food, or tap on a mug with a knife. They also say that the sound of someone coming with food always made Gargantua very happy ... I was thinking about his legendary appetite when I decided to give our big breakfast the name Gargantua. Look at what you have on your plate: sausages, bacon, ham, two eggs, a nice crêpe, tasty *cretons,* baked beans, home fries, and as much toast as you wish. Don't you think it's a breakfast that would be worthy of Gargantua?"

"I'm the giant around here!" shouted Alexandre.

"That's perfect, sweetie; you can decide who you want to be today and who you'll become in the future. It's up to you to find meaning in your life. You can be

Gargantua, and you can be Shakespeare, too, and write the play of your own life."

"Who's Shakespeare, Grandma?"

"Eat your sausages. Shakespeare is another kind of giant you'll learn about later."

"You're Shakespeare, too, Cora," the angel whispered to me. "All the meaning in the world is in your head. You're the one who can choose to be happy, miserable, or a winner; you decide what's best for you."

It suddenly seemed like I had a big box of coloured pencils in my head, and that I was using them to draw my own reality.

"Cora, you need to stop waiting for someone to read the tea leaves before you act. It's up to you to play the main role in your life on earth; you decide what you're going to feel when this or that happens; you chose the reaction you're going to have in any given situation. Pink, black, yellow, red, or navy blue, no colour is better than any other, just like no emotion is better than another; each one is different and appropriate, depending on the outlook or the paintbrush you happen to be using. There's nothing bad in all creation, just love, which always inspires us. And even if the results don't always seem fantastic, that's part of this play called life, too."

***

Like Husserl, the German philosopher I studied in

school, said, we have to go beyond our reality. Thought must be able to go beyond its physical appearance, then rise and contemplate the phenomenon of becoming reality. By looking down from above in this way, the heart-mind-soul trinity can understand that it's greater than any one of the everyday circumstances that occur in its material state, that it's above all of them and has the power to change them. I didn't listen carefully when I was in school, but today, if I went back, my ears would be like satellite dishes trying to capture all the knowledge flying around.

It was time for me to remove the scales from my eyes and start to recognize the multiple processes that are all part of the same thing: everything has contributed to my success. The pitfalls, the elation, the discouragement and the lack of understanding were all part of my journey towards success and heaven.

You can learn public speaking with Dale Carnegie, read the best management theories, study complex accounting systems, recite Warren Buffet's advice from memory, have friends in high places at the Toronto Stock Exchange, or be the finance minister's nephew, but if you don't know it's impossible to fail, you can never completely succeed. When you realize one direction isn't right and the next one isn't really any better, you start thinking all the roads are blocked. I went through that kind of fog, and I never would have remembered I had my finger on the light switch if I hadn't hit my head a few times on the rough walls of despair.

Disappointment is part of success; it's the other side of the coin, and without it, there would be no reward either. We have to learn to throw the coin overboard, and go beyond the limits of our annoyances. And, just like Gargantua, we have to remember that the bigger paradise is, the more love we'll need to put our arms around it; the bigger our success is, the more confidence it will take to feed it.

CHAPTER 66

Listen to the Silence

I'M PROUD TO BE AT THE ORIGIN OF SO MANY MORNING pleasures; proud, too, of everything I learned along the way. In life, it serves no purpose to climb up onto a pedestal; quite the opposite is true, really. You have to fall off your pedestal if you want to be part of the "real world." When you jump off that cliff, you expand, because you learn to move forward in a different way; you have to open a parachute of new ways of doing things. You can't imagine that you're always going to win, and sometimes the opposite of what you imagine turns out to be the best thing for you. Losing a battle is not losing the war, especially when you've got fifty battalions stationed here and there around the province. A torpedo may hit along one of your flanks, or a mudslide may block the horizon. A good general learns from adversity; he continues to advance towards the objective even if, from time to time, a crow makes a deposit on his handsome uniform. We must not bury our talents ten feet underground, or deprive ourselves of the great unused abilities in our heads. The biggest undeveloped territory, as someone once said, lies between our ears.

Finding the answers to business equations is not always as easy as adding two plus two. We can't expect our questions to find a single right answer. You have to let go a little if you're the kind who doesn't want to change the kind of cheese you use in a sandwich. Each day doesn't conclude with a kiss from Prince Charming; you have to expect your dishwasher to quit in the middle of a full house, and you can't be surprised if a plumber forgets to tighten the drain pipe one Friday afternoon. You have to get used to asking instead of giving orders because the new generation wants to work with you rather than feeling like they're your kids and you're forcing them to make their bed. You have to celebrate everything good and make a really big deal out of it, because recognition stimulates performance and because modern executives' instinct is for competition, not standing on the sidelines. You have to watch out for preconceived ideas because, a lot of the time, the Armani suit is not clothing the right body.

You always have to serve top quality food, because that's what brings the customers back to your table. That's what leaves the best taste on the tongue when the stomach is done with the work of digestion. You have to be careful when your business is running full steam ahead because, the faster things are going, the harder it is to see into the distance. You absolutely have to know how to listen to the silence; it often has the most to say concerning things that are important to your organisation. You really become a good boss when no one needs you anymore. But watch out, you can't make the mistake of thinking you're going to work less when you've managed to climb the hill of success; there's always a new city under construction in the head of an entrepreneur.

When I started flipping eggs on the grill at Côte-Vertu, my goal was to feed my children. Then I wanted to have CORAS all over Quebec. Now, the province is full of them, and my goal is to open more restaurants all over Canada. Tomorrow, you can easily guess, the goal will be to move into the U.S. It would be tempting to conclude that my biggest success is finally managing to have a future that is bigger than my appetite to grow.